Praise for **The Oneness Blessing**:

"This book is a MUST-READ! **The Oneness Blessing** miraculously makes previously complex spiritual ideas simple to understand. I felt Deeksha flow through me as I read it and easily returned to the feelings of joy and surrender I felt while at Oneness University in India. The stories in it are amazingly clear and thoughtful, and at the same time, every page has a miracle encoded in it. One can randomly open to any page, and access truth that will set you free. It's a book to be read over and over."

—Mark Anthony Lord, author of *Thou Shall Not Suffer* and creator of PRIDE 2.0., *www.markanthonylord.com*

"A fascinating read! When the world offers daily grim and daunting reports for our future, Ms. Rosenfeld delivers **The Oneness Blessing**—a resource that was for centuries available to only a few in Southern India—connecting us to a power that has the potential to uplift and improve the lives of every person on the planet."

—Sara Connell, author of *Bringing in Finn, Elle* magazine nominee for book of the year in 2012

The Oneness Blessing

The Oneness Blessing

How Deeksha Can Help You Become
Your Authentic Self, Heal Your Relationships,
and Transform the World

Paula Rosenfeld

 New Page Books
A division of The Career Press, Inc.
Pompton Plains, N.J.

THE ONENESS BLESSING
EDITED AND TYPESET BY KARA KUMPEL
Cover design by Dutton and Sherman Design
Printed in the U.S.A.

To order this title, please call toll-free 1-800-CAREER-1 (NJ and Cana-da: 201-848-0310) to order using VISA or MasterCard, or for further information on books from Career Press.

The Career Press, Inc.
220 West Parkway, Unit 12
Pompton Plains, NJ 07444
www.careerpress.com
www.newpagebooks.com

Library of Congress Cataloging-in-Publication Data

Rosenfeld, Paula.
  How Deeksha can help you become your authentic self, heal your relationships, and transform the world / by Paula Rosenfeld.
     pages cm
  Includes bibliographical references and index.
  ISBN 978-1-60163-361-3 (alk. paper) -- ISBN 978-1-60163-391-0 (ebook : alk. paper) 1. Spiritual life. 2. Awareness. 3. Spiritual healing. 4. Enlightenment (Buddhism) 5. Enlightenment (Zen Buddhism) 6. India--Religion. I. Title.

BL624.R673 2015
204'.46--dc23

2015003482

This book is dedicated with love to my daughter, Madeline, my parents, Ruth and Gene, and to my ancestors who may have thought God had abandoned them.

Acknowledgments

I especially honor and offer infinite gratitude to our beloved Sri Amma and Sri Bhagavan, whose magnificent vision and love for humanity is beyond words. I also treasure and give humble thanks to the Guides of Oneness University who inspire, tirelessly teach, and carry the vision of Oneness with grace's perfection. Without the loving support of Guide Doug Bentley, I may never have stepped up to the call of this book. Enormous appreciation goes to Doug and the Oneness Guides for reviewing and approving the contents of this manuscript. Thank you, beautiful beings!

To my dear friends, please know my gratitude for the months I disappeared into my writer's cave while you patiently tended our heart connection. Thank you Savita, Claudia, Betty, Marilee, Scott, Ellen, and all my wonderful sangha soul mates.

My heart is filled with thankfulness for the guidance and light of my first Oneness teachers and friends: Biana, Taz, Kristin, and Mariana. I'm so inspired by the courage, clarity, and strength of your leadership.

Love and thanks to Rev. Mark Anthony Lord and to the Chicago area community of Deeksha Givers for their contributions in grounding the vision of universal oneness. How blessed I am to be part of a dynamic community so dedicated to transformation.

Thank you to Laurie Kelly-Pye and Michael Pye, our insightful co-publishers, for their faith in me, as well as the need for this book. Finally, and so importantly, a huge thanks to the incredible generosity of time and spirit of the Oneness Trainers, whose experiences and wisdom shine through these pages. May their words spark grace and transformation for our readers, as they have for me.

Contents

Imagine

What if you had the opportunity to receive an amazing gift that would help you feel happy, know inner peace, set right your relationships, ease your financial concerns, and live the deeply satisfying life of your dreams? What if this gift came in the simple package of the touch of someone's hands on your head, costing nothing and having no strings attached?

Would you doubt its authenticity? Could you even imagine that something so simple could change your life that dramatically? Well, believe it or not, the gift is called *awakening*, and although it has to be given to you, there is a phenomenon happening on the planet right now that makes awakening available to everybody.

Perhaps, though the gift was offered, you cynically turned away. Perhaps you continued looking for happiness in the bells and whistles of modern life, pursuing, just as I did, such keys to happiness as exotic vacations, fine dining, attractive clothes, and a beautiful home, and all the while half-heartedly squeezing your sparkling life-force energy into a sometimes numbing job in order to bring home a steady paycheck. There's nothing wrong with any of that, but you might find, as I did, that despite all your acquisitions, manifestations, and vacations, there's still a sense of something missing. Maybe there's still a craving within that wants to be filled with something—anything—that will satiate the restless "wanting" of your mind.

I was like that. My mind craved the things my family taught me were desirable. Television, magazines, and popular culture sold me on "the good life" from a very young age. But when I acquired those things, I was still left with inner emptiness.

I had a typical suburban upbringing. My parents raised me to value hard work and success. I was an "A" student, went to a good university, and graduated with honors along with a group of peers in the 1970s who had the brains and the talent to change the world for the better. Yet, as so many of my peers also discovered, the diploma did not lead to happiness. Instead, I faced life with a restless, gnawing yearning. After all that education, I didn't have a clue who I was or how to fit into a world in which I actually felt like an outsider. I wasn't living authentically, wasn't even aware that I wasn't, and could only compare what I mistakenly thought was my identity to the success that others seemed to enjoy. I was plagued by inner conflict. One part of me believed life was meaningless, and another part felt that if only I found the right job, the right life partner, the right home, and the right car, then I would be happy. I spent years searching for happiness in the pursuit of the typical signs of success. My mind kept telling me that I could do better, that what I had in my life wasn't enough. I believed that *I* wasn't enough.

Although I was naturally a very spiritual person from a young age, my version of God was a God who seemed to help *others* find happiness, but not me. My God seemed to be a demanding God who put me through painful tests that I apparently failed. In my mind, something was terribly wrong with me, and I was determined to solve the problem of "me" so that I could finally be happy.

At age 30, I thought, if only I could make some really good money, then I'd be happy; then I'd have security and would find inner peace. So I found work in which I started to make a good income. But it soon became apparent that I wanted something more from life than just a lot of money. So I began to think that if I only got married, then I would be happy. I thought the problem was that I needed to be stable, secure, and "normal" like everyone else.

I soon married a nice man with an up-and-coming career. We bought a lovely home, joined gyms, looked great, had money in the bank, and took resort vacations. However, the satisfaction was fairly short-lived. Eating away at my tentative peace was the thought that if I got pregnant, then I would be happy. It took several years to get pregnant, but in 1987, pregnant I got. Within months of my daughter being born, although I was overjoyed to have her, my marriage became increasingly filled with conflict. I felt lonely. I began to perceive the marriage as unsupportive and unfulfilling. I thought, if only I could find a better-suited partner, then I'd be happier. When our daughter was only 3, we got divorced.

As a single mother, I began dating a long string of people, searching for someone who would be the perfect fit. Along that road, I changed careers, still seeking satisfaction and relief from my restlessness. If I could just fix this discontentment, I thought, then life would be perfect. Then I would be perfect! I got more training, more certifications, and read more self-help books in an effort to find that elusive state of happiness. By the time I was in my early 50s, I was still a single mom, and still a spiritual seeker with a boatload of personal challenges in all of the major areas of my life—health, finances, romance, and, most painfully, a problem trusting a God who brought other people happiness, but not me.

At that time, it felt as if my life was completely falling apart. Internally, there was a sense that I was dying. What was dying was the identity I'd crafted from a lifetime of roles and acquisitions. This came around the same time as the stock market crash of 2008, which really brought my suffering to a head. I was scared, lost, disappointed by life, and still believed that if I could just find true love, change careers again, make more money, and achieve better health, *then* I would be happy. But I had absolutely no idea how to accomplish any of those things, especially in an unstable world where so many financial, governmental, and environmental structures were also crumbling. I felt like a real failure, believing that there was inherently some "success and happiness" gene missing in my DNA.

Several floundering and shaky years passed. One day, I met two young people in their 20's, Taz Rashid and Biana Mavesheva, a radiant couple who changed the course of my life profoundly. They were called Certified Oneness Trainers and they invited me to come experience a Oneness Blessing gathering in Chicago. I had no idea what the Oneness Blessing was, but I went out of curiosity. At that event, I discovered that the Oneness Blessing, also called Deeksha, is a transfer of sacred energy. Deeksha Givers pass the energy by placing their hands on the top of the recipient's head, potentially initiating a process of transformation. The Oneness Trainers explained that this Deeksha is believed to catalyze awakening, which is a neurobiological shift in the brain resulting in reduced stress and enhanced awareness, joy, inner peace, authenticity, and perception of the oneness that animates and unifies all life.

My first Deeksha had a powerfully calming effect, and although I was no stranger to heightened spiritual states, I was surprised to see, with my "inner eye," an odd little golden ball hovering around my forehead during the experience. I was immediately drawn to the Oneness Phenomenon and recognized that it was somehow different from other meditative and consciousness-expanding experiences I'd had in the past, though I couldn't put words to the difference at that time. All I knew was that it felt good, and I really needed to feel good. The Deeksha Giver's hands on my head felt gentle and loving, and left me with a sense of inner peace and safety. It seemed so simple, yet its effect compelled me to want to know more about it and to experience more Oneness Blessings.

I learned that the Oneness Blessing is a phenomenon sweeping the globe now. There are groups of people sharing Deeksha all over the world, including Asia, India, North and South America, Europe, Russia, and Africa. It is nondenominational, requiring no allegiance to any religion, politics, or belief system. One does not have to believe in God, or, if one does, it need not be any certain type of God.

The Oneness Phenomenon is a gift of grace that is changing human consciousness in unprecedented numbers. People in all corners of the world are awakening and becoming liberated from the conflicted mind. They are realizing that their authentic self is not the identity created by the mind. They're observing their thoughts and behavioral patterns with heightened awareness. The Oneness Phenomenon is helping people to have better relationships, to improve their finances, to be more loving, happier, and healthier. It's actually allowing regular, everyday people such as myself, all over the world, to experience many miracles in their lives first hand.

Where this phenomenon comes from is amazing, and you'll find out more about it in this book. But even more important than its origin is the fact that it's here, now, and available to all of us. We needn't look to biblical or mythical stories of miracles, for our modern-day miracles are happening right now, at a time when this planet needs them most.

Many other Oneness Blessings followed my first one. I became an initiated Deeksha Giver myself, then eventually an Awakened Certified Oneness Trainer, and have watched my life turn upside down in a very good way. At first, none of the problems I was having with finances, love, health, or career changed in outer appearances, yet I was increasingly filled with peace, happiness, and faith that things were all right, despite appearances.

My connection to God became passionately alive in my life. I began to believe in a Divine that wanted me to be happy, and to fulfill all the yearning I'd held in my heart for so long. In fact, I felt enlivened and fulfilled in the gifts of the Oneness Blessing.

My craving to be anyone other than myself dropped away. Living in the present moment became enough, and, in fact, filled with perfection. Self-awareness of various aspects of my personalities, thoughts, habits, and judgments became heightened. I accepted and felt gratitude for what used to seem so hopeless and tragic about my life, and instead, saw a loving, sacred hand in it all. I began to accept myself unconditionally, which enabled me to love and accept others unconditionally. Gradually, my health, relationships, career, gratitude, and level of joy have become unmistakably blessed with abundance and renewal.

In this book, you will read about the experiences of ordinary, everyday people whose lives have become transformed by the Oneness Blessing. These are stories of deepened relationships, restored health, newly discovered purpose, unconditional self-acceptance, financial miracles, and more. These are people who stumbled upon happiness in the most unexpected ways through the Oneness Phenomenon. Unconditional peace found them as they discovered for themselves what was uniquely true and transcendent in their lives.

Today, as I write this, I know that my heart has opened wider, as the hole that once kept me restlessly searching for happiness has become filled after awakening. Some days, my chest almost hurts as it stretches to catch the flow of grace pouring into my heart. I am one of millions globally experiencing such abundant grace. We share our stories so that you can find your own way, your own truth, and your own happiness. What you need is only curiosity, openness to transformation, and having a basic sense that there must be more to life than the old ways of obtaining pleasure. Of course, these pleasures can, indeed, be beautiful, important, and are absolutely not to be minimized! Do seek to fulfill your desires. Yet, if you have a deep, restless sense that you are more, and that life is more than the ever-present cravings of your body and the disgruntled running chatter of your mind, then I invite you to read on.

In the following chapters, you'll encounter the words of articulate, awakened, Certified Oneness Trainers, sharing how Deeksha has impacted their own lives and those whom the Oneness Phenomenon has touched. It's been an enormous blessing and an incredible honor to connect with these trainers, whose radiant energies fill this book. Their joy, gratitude, humor, and wisdom inform, lead, and inspire. Each of their voices expresses a unique accumulation of life history, and yet they all share the same universal challenges we all face as human beings: to love and be loved, and to feel significant, happy, healthy, successful, and safe. They give us an amazing glimpse of what it's like to lead an ordinary, yet extraordinary, awakened life.

At the beginning of each chapter, you'll find a teaching from Sri Bhagavan, who, along with his wife Sri Amma, sparked the Oneness Phenomenon and founded Oneness University in India. From September 2010 to July 2014, many of these teachings were posted weekly on the Oneness University Website.

Sri Bhagavan refers to the "Awakened One" and the "un-awakened one" in many of the teachings. When you read this book, you'll better understand what these terms mean. Please know that after awakening, the teachings begin to be *experienced* by those who have awakened. Before awakening, however, the teachings can be used for contemplation; the meanings become alive, and most useful as guidance, after the neurobiological shift in the brain has taken place.

Somehow, this book has found you. If you're feeling skeptical, by all means, have that skepticism. I have skepticism in me too, and also plenty of stubbornness! But if, additionally, you've got curiosity, then I wish you a fantastic adventure exploring the Oneness Phenomenon. If you'd like to try Deeksha, there's a Resource section included at the end of the book for learning more about Oneness University and connecting with trainers near you. All it takes is a bit of willingness for the magic to unfold.

The Oneness Temple at Oneness University, India

CHAPTER 1

The Oneness Blessing: A Global Phenomenon

The Awakened One is free of the mind.
The unawakened one is a prisoner of the mind.
—Sri Bhagavan

Weekly Teachings, Week 137: April 28–May 4, 2013

The Oneness Blessing is possibly the most amazing phenomenon humanity has ever been gifted with. We've certainly received many gifts throughout time, but this beautiful and powerful blessing, also known as Deeksha, is helping humanity become aware of our universal illusion of separateness, the source of our existential suffering. It has the power to make us conscious of our oneness, and not just in words or in concepts; the gift of the Oneness Blessing is the actual living, unfolding experience of what true oneness means.

The suffering experienced by humanity, which has its origin in the illusion of separation, is caused by the mind. The mind is also thought of as the ego. When we are freed from the mind's grip, or as Oneness calls it, "de-clutched" from the mind, we are returned to our natural state of joy and unity. Our hearts flower. We are liberated from the conditioning of the mind, which prevents us from experiencing our own individual truths through the heart and the reality of the present moment.

Sri Amma and Sri Bhagavan are the world-renowned visionaries through whom the Oneness Blessing Phenomenon was birthed in southern India. Sri Amma and Sri Bhagavan are known as avatars—enlightened beings who bring a special gift to humankind. From the time when Sri Bhagavan was a child, it was his deep passion to help individuals lead happy and fulfilling lives. Sri Amma, on the other hand, had a deep passion to marry God and to help with the work. They married in 1976, and together have dedicated their lives to alleviating humanity's suffering by addressing the root cause of the terrible conflict, struggle, and wars between nations and within the human mind.

In 1984, Sri Amma and Sri Bhagavan founded a children's school in southern India called Jeevashram that carried their vision to alleviate human suffering. Their goal was to educate and nurture the natural spirit, intelligence, and consciousness of young people in a holistic manner. Their own son, Krishanji, attended Jeevashram. It was through Krishanji that the Oneness Blessing was first transmitted. One day, a beautiful golden ball of light descended into young Krishanji. This golden ball had manifested to Sri Bhagavan in his childhood through young adulthood. Sri Bhagavan asked Krishanji if he could transfer this golden ball of light to other students. Soon many students were transmitting the golden light; this became the phenomenon known as the Oneness Blessing or Deeksha.

Sri Amma and Sri Bhagavan's powerful vision took hold through the Deeksha, and they began to attract thousands of people to them. They developed a profound body of teachings that also brings forth their visionary intention to end humanity's suffering.

Oneness University

In 2002, Sri Amma and Sri Bhagavan founded Oneness University near Chennai, India, where people now go from all parts of the world to take life-changing courses in consciousness transformation. In 2004, they began offering a Deeksha initiation process through Oneness University that enabled Deeksha to spread to many countries. Soon after, Oneness University began certifying Oneness Trainers who could also initiate Blessing Givers. The beautiful, grace-filled, marble Oneness Temple on campus was completed and consecrated in 2008 after seven years of construction. The Oneness Temple is used for specific ancient processes.

Now, millions of people have experienced the benefits of Deeksha. Certified Oneness Trainers are able to initiate

Deeksha Givers in their home countries across the globe. Oneness Trainers offer many courses and processes that educate, inspire, and support transformation. Krishanji, today, is responsible for the day-to-day operation of Oneness University, its courses, and the outreach programs that are transforming the neighboring Indian villages with humanitarian efforts to improve the health, prosperity, and consciousness of the Indian people. Sri Amma and Sri Bhagavan, so beloved and respected by those who have been blessed by their work, continue to anchor their profound vision, which has spread rapidly across the planet.

Thousands of people are recognizing the Oneness Blessing Phenomenon, regardless of geographical location, religion, or belief systems, because the nature of this transmission is part of every human being's heart. We're all longing for this, whether we're aware of it or not, and it's spreading like wildfire.

A Neurobiological Shift

The transmission of light that is Deeksha is a catalyst for a neurobiological shift in the brain and a rise in awareness of the recipient. This transfer of energy passes through the hands and intention of initiated Deeksha Givers, and through the eyes of initiated Oneness Meditators. The Oneness Blessing is said to deactivate the parietal lobes of the brain, which are responsible for the "fight or flight" response, and activate the brain's frontal lobe. This change in brain function promotes experiences of joy, love, and connection to all. Deeksha supports a process that can lead to a *permanent* experience of inherent oneness, the truth of one's being, which is referred to as permanent "awakening." The rise in awareness associated with Deeksha and awakening means that self-awareness increases and identification with the conditioned mind decreases. As Catherine Scherwenka, an Awakened Advanced Oneness Trainer and Oneness Meditator, explains,

So many of us are living our lives through conditioning and concepts. The conditioning comes from growing up in a family, from your education, from society, from your government, from your country, and from the karma of your country. There are so many layers of conditioning that we all get stuck living in, without awareness. That's a prison of the mind when you don't have awareness. When you're not able to see and be objective about your true reality, then you're living through conditioning; you're living, basically, through the past.

To become free as a human being, it means that the awareness is born and you're able to shine a light upon a conditioning. The conditioning is not going to change, and it's not going to go away. Conditioning is beautiful; that's what creates our world. But instead of living a conditioning without awareness, where you're kind of like a robot going through the motions, when a light is shined upon the awareness, and you're able to see that this is the conditioning, that's the freedom. That's when there's a separation from thinking you are the mind, versus you being an objective witness to the mind and what the mind does.

Deeksha is the light that shines upon awareness. A Deeksha can feel subtle, blissful, or strong, and each Deeksha is experienced as uniquely as is its recipient. The effect of Deeksha is cumulative. One of my first teachers, Kristin Panek, who is an Awakened Advanced Oneness Trainer and Sacred Chambers Facilitator in Downer's Grove, Illinois, notes,

> I see that people participating in my courses and Oneness Blessing evenings begin to get deep insights and begin trusting themselves. They open up and are courageous enough to look honestly at their lives and what's happening for them. If they believe in a Divine or higher creative intelligence, they strengthen that bond with it. This translates to huge transformations in their lives over time.

The Oneness Blessing Phenomenon is not a religion or path. Anyone, from any kind of religious, spiritual, or secular background can receive the benefits of Deeksha. The teachings associated with Oneness are not new, in the sense that they are culled from universal truths that are echoed in many of the world's great teachings and traditions. What makes the Oneness Phenomenon truly unique is the non-denominational Deeksha and the shift in the brain that occurs from receiving the Blessing.

A Miraculous Gift to Humanity

The tradition of Deeksha, which is a Sanskrit term referring to an initiation, can be found deep in the records of Indian culture. Historically, enlightened teachers gave the gift of Deeksha extremely rarely to certain privileged students. As Catherine Scherwenka explains,

> Until now, Deeksha would be given to a student from his teacher only after he had studied and meditated for more than 30 years. Then the student might get one hands-on Deeksha from his teacher. The Deeksha would shift the brain and bring the person closer and closer to enlightenment or awakening. So to have this phenomenon given to the common laypeople, all over the world, is a miracle. In the past, it was a hand-chosen few who got to receive this grace.
>
> The mission of Oneness has always been to awaken humanity back into their natural state of love, connection, peace, joy, and authenticity. Authenticity includes anger, sadness, and pain. Deeksha was given as a tool to awaken us back to the natural, authentic state we were born with.

I think most people's first experience of Deeksha is very peaceful and blissful. It feels peaceful because it quiets the chattering of the mind. It quiets the parietal lobe. I've heard often that the deep sense of peace that one experiences after receiving one's first Deeksha is what brings people back. It's so rare to get into that grounded, quiet space. I believe it gets people attuned with their higher self. It connects them to something so deep that they can't deny it, and they say, "Oh my gosh, what is this?"

The actual transmission of a Oneness Blessing happens very quickly, often in less than a minute's time. Typical Deeksha circles occurring throughout the world offer a recipient numerous Blessings from Deeksha Givers during one gathering. All of the trainers interviewed in this book lead Deeksha circles, teach Oneness courses, and facilitate processes. Some have Oneness centers, where they also host the Three Chamber Process (also called Sacred Chambers). As you continue to read, you will learn more about each of these extraordinary aspects of the Oneness Phenomenon.

Rev. Dr. Michael Milner, an Awakened Advanced Oneness Trainer, Oneness Meditator, and Sacred Chambers Facilitator, has a Oneness center in Florida. His first Deeksha had a life-changing effect on him. This experience illustrates how Deeksha, in addition to offering a taste of bliss, can be a huge catalyst for increased self-awareness. He shares,

After decades as a full-time pastor and spiritual teacher, I had become broken and disillusioned with all organized religions and spiritual movements. I retired from public ministry and went to work as a carpenter for three years. I never intended to be involved in public spiritual work of any kind again. One day, a student of mine came to me, whom I'd been teaching Taoist Meditation to for about 15 years, and he told me about Deeksha. He's a very advanced meditator and a full-time spiritual teacher in his own right. He said, "Michael, I think you need to experience Deeksha."

My wife, Suzanne, and I sat in the living room with this student and we prayed to Sri Bhagavan to show us his stuff. We'd been around the block and I wasn't looking for anything. This idea of enlightening humanity sounded far-fetched, but I thought, "If it's real, then show us."

An amazing energy quickly filled the room and took me into a divine state of consciousness. I didn't care about that; I wasn't looking for that anymore. But after about 20 minutes of this very high, ecstatic state, the Deeksha energy took me deep into my unconscious, integrating into awareness the causes of my suffering and the hidden charges. I thought, "That is so cool. That is it." The heart of the spiritual journey is facing that stuff and bringing it into awareness. I knew from years of contemplative experience that the only way this happens is through Divine grace.

After that night in our living room, I quit working as a carpenter and began to work for Oneness full time, and have continued to this day. It was the experience of Deeksha that led to that shift.

What I see as so wonderful about Deeksha is the way that it is helping people to embrace and fully experience those buried charges. The charges are the bag of pain that keeps us from experiencing the Divine. The charges are the source of all programs that make us feel miserable: "I'm not good enough to be loved. I'll never succeed. I'll never be prosperous." Those programs are being generated by those unconscious charges. They play on and on in the outer life's relentless patterns. I've seen people liberated from that just by the grace of the Deeksha.

In the next chapter, we explore what it means to have unconscious "charges" and how holding "what is" can be the doorway to authentic joy.

CONTEMPLATION

1. Do you believe you are the thinker of thoughts or the one witnessing the thoughts?

2. What repetitive thoughts cycle through your mind regularly?

CHAPTER 2

The Art of Becoming Happier

Any movement away from the "what is" is "suffering."
—Sri Bhagavan

Weekly Teachings, Week 193: May 25–31, 2014

I n the search for happiness, it turns out that the place where happiness lives is as close as the air we breathe. We actually come equipped by nature with the very state we long for. That state, however, is camouflaged by illusions. We take the illusions to be reality and then suffer in our craving for the illusions and our resistance to what is real.

We have created habits and rituals to help ourselves feel better, including using food, alcohol, drugs, work, exercise, sex, and compulsive shopping to numb our emotional reactions to living. We want to run from strong, negative feelings we're having at times, for we fear we can't bear the pain. This creates more unhappiness, a fundamental and ancient condition of being human. These habits of dealing with our feelings seem to temporarily assist us in avoiding feeling bad, but the emotional pain soon resurfaces.

The dominance of the mind has evolved and grown in strength throughout time. The mind would have us focus on what's "out there"—the people, places, and things—rather than the immediate awareness of what's occurring within us in the present moment. Essentially, our mind makes up stories to explain why things happen to us the way they do. The stories come from the conditioning we've had—the concepts fed to us by ancestral and cultural experiences, perceptions, and values.

When we react to something someone said, or a situation that causes us to feel a strong emotion, we tend to point to the external happening as the cause of our internal reaction. In Oneness, having an emotional reaction is often termed "having a charge." We blame or try to change that person, place, or thing that causes the negative charge in us so we can become happy again. If we've lost that elusive happiness (or feel we never had it), it is the nature of the mind to place blame for our unhappiness on something occurring "out there" in the world. The last thing we want to do is to feel the charge, those unpleasant feelings we're having. We try to minimize our suffering by blaming it on someone or something else—our job, our childhood, or our partner, for example. By blaming someone or something for our charges, we continually reinforce our feeling victimized by life. We prolong our pain in this way, never fully processing the emotional charge and just spinning new stories as we focus on others for causing us pain. We live in the clutch of the stories our mind makes up.

In order to move into deeper happiness, we need to bypass the stories that cause us to feel victimized by people and situations and look within to what is really going on. What awakening does is "de-clutch" the mind from its intense grip on non-reality. When the self fully and deeply feels the authentic experience of living, feeling the emotions known immediately through our senses and felt physically in our body, then we flow with the natural energy of life. In the flow, we are not resisting life. It is the resistance to the experiences of our life that causes us pain. Letting go of resistance, we experience fully our emotional reactions and we move through them. When we move through our reactions, we feel happy. It's really quite simple, but it's only when we're awakened that it feels like the most natural thing in the world to do. Until awakening, we are in the clutch of the mind, in the clutch of resistance, and out of the natural flow of life. Before awakening, we need to bring conscious effort to facing our feelings. This is an extremely difficult endeavor.

Staying With the "What Is"

In Oneness, being aware of the energy of the present moment is called "staying with the what is," or "holding."

That is how we practice the art of becoming happier. Within the flow of "what is" is divine, sentient consciousness. It's energetically palpable, knowable, experiential, and eternally unfolding. In the "what is," we may experience The Presence. The Presence is that infinite, supreme intelligence, both in us and around us. We are that. When we are in this state of being, we are consciousness itself, and thus self-aware. Awakening is a shift that allows you to stay with the actual "what is," freed from the grip of a story-making mind. When awakened, there is awareness of reality.

This aspect of awakening is what makes it so ordinary, yet so extraordinary a state. It turns out that ordinary reality, the very thing many of us go to great lengths to avoid, is where the magic of life exists. This is where happiness is found, where life flows, and where acceptance, inner peace, and connection reside.

Mary O'Neill, an Awakened Advanced Oneness Trainer living in California, shares how she has experienced tremendous transformation after being introduced to the Oneness Blessing. She was able to break through her resistance to feeling her long-repressed and destructive emotional pain. As she became more aware of her resistance to feeling her pain, and to stay with the "what is," her life changed dramatically:

> In 2010, I was facilitating an event with a personal growth organization that put me in massive pain. I was leading a weekend workshop with some others and it triggered memories from my childhood. It felt like the people on my team were similar

to my own brothers and sisters. I felt like the people who were supposed to be supporting me were attacking me. I felt betrayed. It was a nightmare.

I remember sitting in the bathtub and just crying. The sadness and pain wouldn't stop. I couldn't turn it off, and this pain just wouldn't leave. I went to a two-day Oneness Awakening Course with a friend. The energy was really strong. I remember during the teachings and some of the processes at the course, I just sat there bawling! I can remember the deep pain in my chest.

At that time in my life, I was distracting myself with watching television and over-eating food, which was the strongest addiction that I used to numb myself. If I had too strong an emotion, I also had to find a friend to talk to. I just couldn't be with myself. I felt so much anxiety when I turned inward. I couldn't stay with what was going on inside me. The physical sensation of my being was this painful anxiety and I couldn't bear it.

At the Oneness Awakening Course that Mary attended, she became aware of how the mind powerfully hijacks our ability to completely feel the fullness of our emotions. That is the mind's nature. Its primary function is to ensure our survival by being in control. Never underestimate the creativity of the mind to steer one away from the physical sensations of our emotions!

When the mind takes control, our attention moves to daydreams, stories, what happened in the past, or what could happen in the future. Our thoughts take us out of what is happening right now. The energy of current emotions becomes trapped in our bodies, as the mind does its best to resist feeling them. The charge of these unprocessed feelings is like a time bomb, waiting to be set off by someone's chance remark, or a situation at work, or something that triggers the pain we've been trying to avoid. Until the feelings can move freely through our body, we're stuck in discomfort or pain. Mary found that receiving the Oneness Blessing supported her in turning inward and releasing her pain:

The teaching that really helped me is to "stay with the 'what is.'" That felt very true to me and was the right direction. The only thing to do is to be with the feelings and let them burn off. When I came to that Oneness Awakening course, I was pretty desperate. Everything I was hanging my hook on to be successful was being pulled away. Anything in my life that I was defining myself as—my job, my relationships—all this was being pulled away. I thought I was a horrible person, that no one would ever love me, no one would ever want to work with me. I had come up against a pattern that was a repeat from childhood. I felt 100-percent discouraged that I could ever change. I thought my life would be this failure.

With the Oneness Blessing, Mary discovered that when she did not resist her feelings, and stayed with them, they would transform. Underneath the emotional pain, there was joy. She felt a sense of support from Deeksha that permitted her to move through her resistance to a much happier state:

> After that, I went to as many Oneness Blessing events as I possibly could. I would receive or give the Blessing, and I was able to be with my feelings because it was as though I had the support of the Blessing. I couldn't have done it by myself. By myself, my mind would come in and I would dart away. I would go into a story about the situations. But in the Blessing events, it was a relief to not run away. I spent months doing this, and it got less over time. The charges gradually got smaller.

As Mary continued to experience the Oneness Blessing Phenomenon, she began to become more aware of how the racing mind distorts and resists reality and keeps us from being present in the "what is." Mary made a big decision:

> I got clear that I could do this work piecemeal, or I could go to Oneness University in India and do it all at once. I looked at other people doing other spiritual practices (not Oneness), and I saw they were still in pain and weren't able to move through

their patterns. So I decided to go to India and I
did two Deepening courses at Oneness University,
back to back. I needed something where I could go
and the whole intention was to not move away at all
from my feelings, but to stay with them. It gave me
the support I needed to release all those charges.

Mary's journey with the Oneness Blessing Phenomenon
has resulted in a permanent shift into awakening. As with
others who are awakened, her brain has undergone a neurobiological change in which the "fight or flight" centers
have become less active. She still has times of feeling emotional pain, but her mind is not in charge; it has been "de-
clutched," as Oneness would describe it. She has less resistance to reality. In non-resistance, there is acceptance of
one's self and others. There is inner peace and joy.

Mary is now able to see her thoughts come and go. She
is aware of having thoughts and generally does not identify
with the mind's stories. She can fully experience her authentic feelings and is able to move through her charges at
a much faster rate than before. This is how she describes the
change in self-awareness and the emotional freedom that
awakening has brought:

After awakening, my awareness is amazing
now. I see things, like memories for instance, that
might hold a charge, but they move quickly; I don't
get caught in any memories. Now, I occasionally
experience resistance, but it's very short. I feel as

though I live "inside" and come out. Before, I could never go inside and I was bouncing around out here.

There is a flow of my awareness of myself in the present moment. There is more integrity and freedom in the way I see myself. All the self-images I had of being a nice person, or a good person, I didn't realize it, but they were imprisoning me. Anything that didn't come under my definition of nice or good, I had to hide from myself. It took so much effort to see the thing that was outside of that definition.

Now, I can see when I'm really jealous of a person, or I hate that person because he or she wasn't nice to me.... I don't need any justification, or saying "he should have done this" or "she should have done that." I can just be honest about it to myself.

There's more freedom and more space for me. It's cool to just see the awareness. It's like a game, the best game ever. I just see where I fool myself and laugh at myself. I feel more space in me to acknowledge publicly what everyone else already knows—that I'm in reaction—instead of trying to hide or pretend. It feels like there's an unwinding in progress of all these images and identities. I don't know if it will ever end, and it doesn't even matter.

As we are able to be more fully in the present moment, to stay with the "what is," the change in our inner world is reflected in the outer world. We become part of the natural flow of life, which is all about change and transformation. Mary describes a huge gift of transformation that unfolded in her relationship with her father as she has taken her inward journey with Oneness:

> A true miracle that's occurred in my experience with the Oneness Blessing is the change in my relationship with my father. I had a childhood with physical and emotional violence in my relationship with him. Even 15 years in therapy didn't remove the deep, ingrained anger I felt toward him. In fact, I defined myself as being a victim of his abuse. But I no longer see myself or him that way.
>
> I had a shift in my feelings toward my father. I have so much more compassion for him. I can say for the first time, I really feel love for my father. I just can't see him the way I used to see him. I still have "stuff" with him, but I see that a lot of the stuff that really annoys me about him is actually stuff that I do, that I modeled after him...I am so humbled.

In the chapter that follows, we'll explore more about the significance of relationships within the Oneness Phenomenon. Relationships are a powerful component of our happiness. But first, direct your focus on your inner self. Before the shift of awakening, this takes much effort.

Receiving and giving the Oneness Blessing supports this effort immensely. After awakening, it becomes the most natural thing in the world to turn inward and stay with the "what is." In fact, it's much harder to avoid it than to stay with it. Awakened or not, the way to move into deeper joy is by allowing our feelings to be experienced fully.

How to Practice the Art of Becoming Happier

1. Become aware of your resistance to painful feelings. When your mind is complaining about something that happened or is happening, you are in a state of resistance.

2. Remind yourself that there is nothing wrong with what is going on inside you. It's really okay to relax your resistance to it and to feel it.

3. Sit down to be with the feelings. Focus on your breathing, allowing it to slow down. Keep your spine erect and turn inward to feel your emotions. Keep breathing!

4. Ask yourself where in your body you are feeling discomfort related to your resistance of the pain. Go deeply into those parts of the body, staying with various sensations if the areas of discomfort shift. Breathe into the sensations.

5. If your mind tries to take you out of it and resistance returns, just notice that, without judgment, and gently return to experiencing what's

inside. At some point, or after repeated sessions, the pain will dissolve into joy.

As you practice staying with your feelings, you become more and more aware of the activity of the mind. After awakening, your mind loses its grip and your heart flowers. Your self-awareness and self-acceptance grow. You will see your life transform as your happiness deepens.

As a powerful practice, you might try sitting down and experiencing your feelings as a daily meditation. This is much easier after awakening, when you find that staying with the "what is" becomes a natural part of your everyday life. If you are now awakened, you're likely experiencing the joy that is possible when we no longer move away from the "what is" and fully experience feelings. As Oneness teaches, anything experienced to completion transforms to joy.

CONTEMPLATION

1. Have you acquired habits or rituals that serve to numb uncomfortable or painful feelings?

2. Have you become aware of any tendencies to blame other people or situations for your own unhappiness?

CHAPTER 3

Healing Relationships

The Awakened One is free of the past.
The unawakened one is a prisoner of the past.
—Sri Bhagavan

Weekly Teachings, Week 119: December 23–29, 2012

Oneness University teaches that life *is* relationships. Making relationships a priority in our life is crucial, for who are we without our relationships? Our world cannot feel right to us unless we are in right relationship with our self, our parents and family, our ancestors, our friends, our coworkers, and all with whom we connect in our lives. If any of these relationships are troubled and conflicted, then our inner peace and connection to all is eroded.

I used to have such a different view of life. I rarely prioritized extended relationships, because I was confused about how they fit into my life. I was conflicted about who would or wouldn't drain my energy and whom I could trust with my heart. This fear and confusion created much needless isolation and loneliness for me. Becoming part of a local Oneness community with others who were experiencing Deeksha and hearing the Oneness teachings showed me a whole new way to be in relationships. I feel so grateful that the first Oneness trainers I met, Biana Mavasheva and Taz Rashid, really modeled authenticity, open-heartedness, and acceptance. This created such a beautiful sense of safety that, as I kept coming back for Deeksha, I began to have glimpses of what it is like to have a real heart connection to others. After awakening, my capacity for true heart-to-heart connection expanded dramatically.

My teacher, Biana Mavesheva, an Awakened Advanced Oneness Trainer, had experienced a similar change in the valuing of relationships through the Deeksha events and teachings. This is how she and many other Oneness trainers are able to facilitate a powerful environment for growth in relationships. She says,

> One of the quintessential teachings of Oneness is that "life equals relationships." That teaching absolutely transformed my life. Now I put

relationships at the top of my priorities. I saw that if I wanted the quality of my life to improve, I had to improve the quality of my relationships. I put in more conscious effort to heal all my relationships, and life responded. Now my life is so much easier. It's filled with more peace, more laughter, and greater communication because my relationships are healthy and fulfilling.

What truly inspires me about Oneness today is the community; seeing people grow over the years...there's a tremendous realness that's present in friendships within the community because we understand that, at the core, we're one. We're supporting each other in growth, and holding each other in a genuine space of caring.

I see our Oneness community growing in consciousness, able to relate to each other from this intimate place of seeing each other as spirit. Humanity is craving to return back to these meaningful connections. We've lost this experience of connection because we identify with the mind's "commentator" that's telling us who the other person is without actually experiencing him or her. Oneness allows us to truly experience the other, and when we do that, the mystical returns.

Look Inward First

We begin to heal our relationships by looking inward first. By staying with the "what is," as we discussed in the previous chapter, we gain clarity about what we are bringing to our relationships. We see that we are often bringing conditioning, reactivity, judgment, blame for our own unprocessed pain, and elaborate stories created by the mind that keep us feeling victimized by others. The practice of staying with the "what is" leads, ultimately, to seeing that each of us holds both positive and negative feelings and traits within our personalities. We reject some aspects of our inner world outright, and instead of taking ownership of these things, we blame others for our misery. We judge and take a self-righteous stance. We think, "Wow, is she messed up. I'm glad I'm not like her!" Or we think, "Gosh, if he would only change, I would be so happy!"

When we awaken and can really *see* the way we operate in relationships, and when we become aware that we can be just as self-absorbed, greedy, defensive, and judgmental as the next person, we gradually come to unconditionally accept all parts of our self. It's then, when we are free of our painful *self*-judgment, that our hearts flower and we can unconditionally love our self and others.

Unconditional Love

Until we awaken, we are in resistance mode. We can't honestly say that we unconditionally love another, though we *think* we do, when we are so busy (subtly and not-so-subtly) resisting our loved ones. We have very little experience with loving through the level of the heart, as opposed to the mind. The fear of being hurt is so strong that we unconsciously experience interpersonal connection through the mind. The mind's desire to avoid pain is that strong.

After awakening, we can truly connect with another through the heart, which knows oneness, not separation. When the conflicted mind loses its grip, the illusion of separation from another person and from all life drops away. An open heart is a beautiful gift of awakening to what is real. With a wide-open heart, and with grace, we flow beyond the conflict, blame, and pain, bringing our authentic self to relationships. With an open heart, we come to experience the oneness of darkness and light—both aspects of wholeness.

Sheri Greenstreet, an Awakened Advanced Oneness Trainer, expresses so beautifully how self-reflection and awakening have gifted her with giving up resistance to accepting and loving herself:

> I was finally able to quit resisting what I was. I accepted what I had become and the life I had created by my own choice. I found that all of my suffering was caused by my steady resistance to my life and to my life experiences. I was an expert resister. I didn't know how to allow love from others or love of self. I resisted that I was playing the victim in my life. I accepted that I didn't know how to let go of resistance. I didn't know how to quit

resisting what I didn't like. It was an exhausting way to live.

Finally, a subtle power came forward from within. Truth is, there's a place inside me that knew what to do at each step of my awakening. From this tiny place within me, I found the ability to completely and unconditionally forgive myself. I discovered love for myself, which eventually led to the doorway where unconditional love, joy, and freedom awaited me. I finally loved me for what and who I was in the present condition I was in, not for what I wanted to or believed myself to be.

Sheri goes on to describe how awakening enabled her to reconcile life's apparent polarity and see the oneness of all her life experiences:

Today, I experience a vast inner quietness. There is a physical and mental stillness in the place of the worry and resistance that was. I see the divine as everything and the interconnectedness of all life. There is a sense that I have played every role over time. I cannot judge another, for I would be judging myself.... Earth in 3D is a life of duality. How would I understand or be able to experience myself as both loving and loved if I didn't know the opposite? I have learned what real love isn't. I have experienced the opposite of feeling safe, feeling peace, stillness, freedom, and bliss. I have fully experienced shame and unworthiness. First the yin, then the yang; one without the other is impossible to understand in duality. I fully recognize and understand unconditional love, allowance, lightheartedness, forgiveness, joy, and bliss; I fully experienced fear, lack, and existing in survival mode.

Healing Relationships with Our Parents

For many, the seeking of joy, peace, and wholeness has kept us hungrily chasing after people and things that could heal our emotional wounds and fill us with the love we deeply desire. Yet, most of us have experienced deep hurt in our relationships, particularly in our childhoods. Hurt blocks our ability to receive love. We carry the hurt around for years and years, both unconsciously and consciously. The old hurt is like chains that bind us to the past and distort our perception of the present.

Of all the human relationships we have, the ones with our parents are the most fundamentally significant. These parent–child relations have the ability to create a positive experience of life, as well as create wounds so deep that the hurt can stay with us for a lifetime. Oneness teaches that our relationships with our mothers and fathers (or the people who acted in those roles in our lives) can affect our prosperity, health, and interactions with others, as well as our bond to whatever we think of as greater than ourselves, such as God or the Universe. Old hurts, unresolved issues, distance, rejection, or chronic conflicts with our parents, whether our parents are alive or have transitioned, can create unconscious obstacles to our success, wealth, health, spiritual growth, and happiness.

Consequently, to live a positive life of contribution, growth, and joy, we need to look within first, to see where we've been hurt by our parents and also see where we have hurt them. The outer world reflects the inner world; if we change our inner world by releasing the inner hurt many of us carry around from childhood, we can impact our outer world. We also need to see that *hurt* is a two-way street.

For so long, I felt victimized by my parents and childhood circumstances. Although my parents are wonderful people who were always trying to do their best, I was unable to see that the personality patterns I developed to protect my vulnerability actually caused pain to my parents. Emotionally armored, I unconsciously avoided responsibility for the hurt I inadvertently caused, due to my own judgment, stories, projection, and reactivity.

What tremendous grace that brought awakening and Oneness tools and teachings into my life, leading me from isolation to connection! Staying with the "what is" is a primary process that enables us to move into the heart by fully *experiencing* the hurt we have received, as well as the hurt we have caused in others. Doing this creates a shift from conflict to heart-centered connection. When one can *feel* as another feels, judgment and defensiveness are replaced by connection, forgiveness, and acceptance.

Forgiveness

Rev. Dr. Patricia Keel, Awakened Oneness Trainer, Oneness Meditator, and Sacred Chambers Facilitator, talks about the way Oneness teaches forgiveness:

> One of the things I really loved about my most recent visit to Oneness University was their teaching on forgiveness, which is to put yourself in the shoes of someone you may have hurt. That has been a huge blessing for me to do that and to feel what someone I may have hurt has felt. That has been a huge heart-flowering experience. That's a beautiful part of what we've been invited into with this phenomenon that we call Oneness. It's taking the teaching and holding it inside, and allowing the grace of the light, or your higher power, or whatever it is you call it, to soften you into that space of feeling someone else.

A really extraordinary occurrence of the Oneness Phenomenon is that the teachings become actual experiences as you move deeper into awakened states or full awakening. Many traditions teach forgiveness, but in Oneness, the teaching of forgiveness becomes alive, and forgiveness can be an effortless happening when you are in a higher state of consciousness and grace is flowing. In fact, in a high state of awakening, one ultimately knows on every level that there is nothing to forgive. But even in the initial stages of the shift into awakening, incredibly profound transformations can occur.

A Sacred Chambers Miracle

The Oneness courses, Oneness Meditations, and, especially, visiting the Sacred Chambers (which I'll discuss more fully later in this book) offer the possibility for dramatic and miraculous change. Believe it or not, I attended one Sacred Chambers session that completely altered my relationship with my mother, allowing me to fully experience her with an understanding that went far beyond the mind.

Even after awakening, I still held a desire to feel closer to my mother, for, if truth be told, I thought we were so different that being close might be an impossibility. She is an avowed agnostic and I am very spiritual, and because of that we've always had difficulty relating to each other's interests and beliefs. As a result, and in my *projection* of my own pain onto her, I felt unloved, unseen, misunderstood, and different. I carried a cumbersome bag of hurt and victimization around into adulthood. This made me sad and influenced my other relationships and situations.

One day I went to the Sacred Chambers in Downers Grove, Illinois, which is a Chambers known to specialize in healing relationships, facilitated by trainer Kristin Panek. I went in with the prayer to feel deeper love and connection with my mom. At that time, I had visited this particular Sacred Chambers three times, and each time, it had been an intensely moving event for me. Each time, I'd had a profound sense of what is sacred and mystical to me. But this time, I was completely surprised by the flatness of my feelings in the Chambers.

The Sacred Chambers comprise three separate rooms. When you arrive, you go into the first chamber, a room that is used for contemplation. There, I felt no sense of the sacred, despite the lovely candles, beautiful artwork, and the different symbols of various religions and traditions that grace an altar. Instead, I saw only chairs, a room, and pictures; I experienced no other dimension but material existence. There was a strange sense of something being missing, which I soon understood to be spiritual in nature. I couldn't feel the powerful love of the Divine that I usually feel in that chamber. Try as I might, I couldn't change my baffling, different experience in this first chamber.

After a while, I was called to go into the second chamber. Again, I felt something missing; there was just a sense of flatness to everything. In the third chamber, the same flatness continued. Finally, back in the first room for the integration time, my inner knowing delivered a huge surprise: with clarity, I suddenly understood that what I had been experiencing was my mother's consciousness. It was, indeed, vastly different from mine. By grace, I had been given the experience of not feeling close to God. Furthermore, I received guidance about the ancestral lineage of her agnosticism, which, as a Jewish lineage, lies in the unconscious feelings of abandonment by God.

I inherited the same lineage, and, seeing this, I better understood my own repressed inner conflict about God. I remembered from my childhood hearing many stories of Jewish persecution throughout history, both from my religious education and my parents. I recalled my mother arguing many times with me, and still to this day, "How can there be a God who would let all those people die in the Holocaust? How can there be a God who allows such suffering in the world?" As a child, I never had a good response to that question. I've grown up so differently from the way my mother did, a child of immigrants who had fled persecution in their home countries.

This event of *experiencing* her consciousness completely opened my heart as I let go of the need to argue my position with her. I could stop blaming her for my own pain of feeling different. I don't have to change her and I no longer take our differences *personally*. Her disagreement with my beliefs is no reflection on me, and having this awareness was the key to releasing the loop of reactive judgment that kept me pushing her away. I no longer feel unloved, for that had been a very old story I'd made up based on distorted childhood assumptions and illusions. That illusion was lifted right out of me when I was able to walk in her shoes. I was able to accept that neither of us is wrong or right. Each of us is perfect, just as we are. I feel her love for me in a way I never could before. I call that experience *grace in action*.

Since that day, I chuckle at the resistance I held for so long to embracing my mother as she is, and taking her ways of being so personally. The audacity of my judgments and the poignancy of projection are obvious to me now, and yet this is how the mind in each of us works. This is what causes so much suffering in relationships and in the world. The lifting of illusions like this is the liberation and healing that we need and long for so desperately.

An Entire Family Heals Through Oneness

Catherine Scherwenka, an Awakened Advanced Oneness Trainer and Oneness Meditator, tells an inspiring story about the childhood pain she and her family experienced and the healing through Oneness courses that rippled through her entire family:

> My parents got divorced when I was 11 years old, in the late '70s or early '80s, when divorce wasn't as common. My mom left my dad, and left him with three of the five children who were still living at home. My dad worked full-time, and felt victimized and hurt by what happened. It was traumatic on many levels.
>
> For many years, my parents were cordial to each other at family gatherings, but there was a lot of deep resentment, maybe even hatred, especially from him to her. Our family has done many, many different kinds of therapies. My dad was in Alcoholics Anonymous, my mother in Al Anon, and we were in Alateen. That program saved our lives, probably, as did all of the different therapies that many of us tried throughout the years to deal with the hurt and pain of what had happened.
>
> So we were all maintaining, I would say, but there was still deep hurt and pain inside that was

61

not getting expressed or experienced. Some years ago, I taught a Oneness Awakening Course that both my parents attended. My Dad's new wife was there, and my brother and his wife were there too. It was kind of a family affair. My whole family has become involved in Oneness, which is a huge gift. So at this Oneness Awakening Course, when you go through the two-day processes, you might have a deep, liberating experience where you actually feel the hurt and pain that was caused to you. You might also feel the hurt and pain you caused others throughout your lifetime. Both my parents went through these processes.

After the Oneness Awakening Course finished, I was hugging and saying goodbye to everyone. I turned around and in front of me were my mother and my father both sobbing and crying, holding each other's arms and staring into each other's eyes. My stepmother was standing right beside them, crying too. It was profound in such a deep way, and healing, on so many levels, for my family. It created so much beautiful space in our family, again. There's a lot more heartfelt connection and authenticity. It doesn't feel like there's all this hurt and pain that's being carried from 30 years ago. Instead, the pain has been moved and released, and now we're all starting to experience reality as it is. I couldn't ask for anything more! It was magical.

In Oneness, it is said that the most important thing is healing the relationships with your mother and father. I do think it is the most important thing in all of our work to make sure those relationships are really strong, full of love, and without a lot of resentment, judgment, and hate. The more we can work through all of that, the better all your relationships in your life will be. You'll be freer as a human being.

CONTEMPLATION

1. Think of the quirks, habits, and traits you dislike in your loved ones. Then ask yourself if you, too, have any of those same qualities or habits. Stay with the feelings that come up.

2. What are you most ashamed of about yourself? Are you willing to ask a Higher Intelligence to help you accept it?

CHAPTER 4

Awakening to the Divine Within

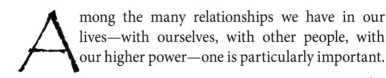

The Awakened One is one with that which was there before the universe was born. It is the one which is eternally present, the unborn and the undying, one without a beginning and an end, ever unchanging, solitary, empty, infinite, blissful, the eternal "I."

—Sri Bhagavan

Weekly Teaching, Week 13: December 12–18, 2010

Among the many relationships we have in our lives—with ourselves, with other people, with our higher power—one is particularly important.

65

Imbedded in the distinctive DNA we carry and influenced by our cultural, ancestral, religious, parental, national, or educational conditioning, this relationship is fundamental to our essence: at the core of our existence, we are each part of the one, universal, creative energy that animates this experience of living.

How we relate to this universal energy, whether consciously or unconsciously, and what we call it, will be singularly personal for each of us. Some may call this universal energy "God" or use another word to describe it. Others don't see it that way and relate to it differently. Many people experience their connection to the universal through nature or artistic expression. Yet, despite all these differences, most people would agree that there exists a huge mystery that is central to life. When we become conscious that we are living within a mystery, we begin to see that we have a relationship with this mystery.

Many Names, One Universal Essence

One of the things I honor and love about the Oneness Phenomenon is that it doesn't ask us all to act the same or to follow one set of beliefs. The phenomenon of Deeksha has no concern for whether or not we believe in God, or some kind of divine force. We can be atheists, agnostics, non-theists, devoutly religious, spiritual but not religious, and everything in between. Deeksha does not interfere with anyone's religion or faith; in fact, it will connect you even more strongly to your religion of choice, if you have one.

66

Science, history, philosophy, and the arts have alluded to the fact that we are of the same eternal essence; we are one essence, and it lives within each of us. The process of awakening to that mysterious universal essence which has been there all along *is* the journey of awakening that Deeksha catalyzes.

Science tells us that are made of energy. Quantum physics theorizes that energy expresses as particles and waves. What we know about energy is still being explored, but if you're like me, perhaps the only thing you really know with relative certainty is what you know through your own experience and senses. In Oneness, there is complete freedom and encouragement to have your own experience. In fact, one thing that makes the Oneness Phenomenon distinctive is that it offers a consistently personal sensory experience. With direct sensory experience, we come to really know what is uniquely true for each one of us.

For example, when I was 18, I had a cherished experience that showed me something about who I am in a direct, undisputable way. At the time, I was home from college, on holiday break. I'd gone down to the beach on Lake Michigan to goof around on a cold, wintry night with my boyfriend of those years. The two of us were alone on the beach and I began to run down the frozen lakefront, feeling a giddy sense of freedom and joy. All of a sudden, time seemed to literally stand still. That sounds like a cliché, but it was true. I was immersed in a deep stillness. I looked around and didn't see my boyfriend. All I saw was the lake and the dark, frozen mounds of sand surrounding me. It felt like I'd stepped off the Earth and entered a different dimension. I later understood that I had spontaneously gone into a heightened state of consciousness, or what Oneness might call an awakened state.

In that expanded, surreal moment, I had a sudden, powerful *knowing* that I was like a wave in the beautiful body of Lake Michigan in front of me. I saw that, in this lifetime, I would peak like a wave and then I would return to that vast body of water from which I came. I was both the wave and the body of water, unique and also inseparably, eternally one with all the other droplets of water and waves. This beautiful knowing indelibly graced me with a fleeting experience of oneness. I have no idea how long that experience lasted in Earth time. As quickly as it came, it left, and I saw my boyfriend walking along the beach again.

From that day onward, I was hyper-charged with a strong yearning to feel that awareness again of the eternal, mysterious essence in which I exist. I was officially launched as a spiritual seeker of a direct *experience* of the Divine. The type of religion I was raised in, Reform Judaism, didn't emphasize *direct revelation of God*, though there is plenty of reference to it in the Bible. I just didn't know, until that day, that it was available to everyone.

As a youngster in religious school, there was much I had found beautiful in Judaism, and some I struggled with. But one of the biggest hurdles for me was that the God I was taught in childhood felt more like a punishing God than a loving God. He was a God who judged the merits of those who didn't follow the customs and commandments. For various reasons, *especially* my own mental projection of shame, I felt quite defective according to the standards set by the God of my youth. Undoubtedly, I must have held an unconscious belief that because God seemed to be extremely wrathful at times, as noted in the Bible, I probably couldn't trust Him and had better flee while I could. Was this similar to the God of your childhood?

In my 20s, after I left my parents' home, I explored other great spiritual traditions in search of a direct experience of God. Other religions and paths had other intriguing names for God: Great Spirit, Universal Intelligence, Holy Spirit, Higher Self, Allah, Light, Brahman, the Universe, and Soul. These words offered more hope to me of finding whatever form of spirituality would feel *experientially* right, uniquely for me. Little did I realize that the judgmental version of God was lingering in my unconsciousness mind. So I fled the fearful version of God and investigated Buddhism, Hinduism, and Christianity. I also explored Jewish mysticism through the Kabbalah. Though the search led me into fleeting, light-filled states of transcendence, my longing for union with the Divine was never satisfied. I found my most fulfilling spiritual affinity within my love of nature and shamanism, but that sense of an inner craving stubbornly persisted.

As time went on I became drawn into all the trappings and allures of adulthood, and spirituality took a back seat for a while. My friends were immersed in careers and marriage. Somehow I forgot I was seeking God and instead I sought transcendence through human love. I kept longing to merge with *someone* who would make me feel completely and unconditionally loved and one with everything. I kept looking for someone to fill the inner emptiness until I happened upon the Oneness Phenomenon and eventually became awakened. Once I got involved in Oneness, it became clear to me, finally, that no person or possession would ever be able to fill that inner longing because it wasn't a person or material thing that I was looking for; it was my Divine, whom of course had been with me all that time. I just didn't know it.

At the first Oneness course I took, the trainers directed my gaze inward and invited me to look at that relationship I had abandoned so long ago—the God of my childhood. It didn't have to be called *God*, they said, for that term is one of many that refer to that which is sacred, fundamental, eternal, whole, within us, surrounding us, ever- and all-present, and of a higher intelligence than our small ego-minds. No matter what it's called, it's the one essence. It lives in us and we live in it. It's that remembering of our essence for which our hearts are yearning.

Oneness generally refers to it as *your personal Divine*, or *Purushothama*, or the *Antaryamin*; these last two terms come from Indian spiritual traditions. Because Oneness University is in India, those terms are often heard there, but essentially, these are only names for a relationship with our sacred essence, a universal consciousness. Oneness tells us to look within for this, and encourages us to develop a close, deeply bonded relationship with this living consciousness, using whatever name we wish to call it. When we give this living essence a name and an image, it becomes much easier to relate to it.

The Power of Personal Experience

Many spiritual traditions and religions invite us into inner contemplation, devotion, and union with that which we consider sacred. The Oneness Blessing itself, as well as other Oneness practices, makes these states uniquely accessible by being personally and directly experiential. Certified Oneness Trainer and Sacred Chambers Facilitator Cynthia Lamborne explains:

> I reflect occasionally on what was pulling me along all this time. The pull for me since the late '80's was this longing for intimacy with the All That Is. That is what pulled me to take a lot of human development training such as meditation. I understood that it feels so intimate within myself to connect deeply in a meditation. Wow, to share that kind of quality with another person through Deeksha is a very profound experience for me.
>
> During one intense experience at Oneness University, something opened in my heart. I had a vision of my Higher Self as a glowing, physical being. In my immediate experience of the vision, I didn't have words for it and I didn't have a part of my brain that could even cognize that this was really happening. But my heart took over and there was a deep knowing of its truth. As a Sacred Chambers facilitator, I often see that some people don't seem to have something in the brain to even cognize what has happened. That's why it's so important to hear other people's experiences. And the

Deeksha is so important because it actually starts rewiring the brain to hold this new awareness.

The sacred energy that is Deeksha supports a rising in awareness of our essence. As I continued to receive and give Deeksha, take Oneness courses, and grow in self-awareness, the unconscious concepts and repressed emotions I held in regard to my relationship with God became clearer and clearer. The heightened self-awareness released many blockages and illusions, and allowed reality to reveal itself. I began to see and feel life differently, and experienced the energy of a Higher Intelligence, of my inner Divine, in a direct, lasting, real, and personalized way.

Awakened Advanced Oneness Trainer, Oneness Meditator, and Sacred Chambers Facilitator Rev. Dr. Michael Milner says about this personal connection with your own Divine:

People can decide what gift or grace they want to relate to the Divine. There's this incredible energy that restructures the brain physiology. It opens the door to higher states of awareness, and that's awesome. It becomes evident in time that this is the Divine Presence itself. Eventually we're living in it 24/7. At some point, it becomes our personal Divine. We discover there's an aspect of the Divine that Oneness University always called "personal Divine," but not everyone always understood what that meant.

What it means is that there is an aspect of the Paramatma (the Divine) that lives in you and me, which is all about you and me 24 hours a day, 7 days a week. For any person who discovers this relationship, he or she is able to have what the human heart has always been longing for: Someone that just cares about me and thinks about me all day and all night. It's maybe what some of us thought we wanted in a romantic relationship and soon discovered that was never going to happen! There's no one who is only going to care about me 24 hours a day, except this Paramatma. So we can look forward to having the most amazing relationship that we ever dreamed of having.

As we develop intimacy with our Divine within, this personal aspect of the All That Is, we begin to transform at rapid speeds. Rev. Dr. Michael goes on to say,

Initially, happiness is the indicator of spiritual growth, and, yes, people are becoming happier. People are coming to an acceptance of themselves. Relationships are being transformed. Whole families are being transformed. Transformation includes so much more: The flowering of the heart and the beginnings of opening to higher states of consciousness.... As our hearts flower in transformation, we experience deeper and deeper levels of connection with others, and genuine compassion begins to flower.

Grace

The effect of Deeksha to support an awakening to the Divine within is cumulative. Additionally, Oneness University and trainers offer courses and practices to nurture the direct *experience* of your personal Divine. In addition to receiving Deeksha, one of the most powerful ways to have a direct, personal experience is by visiting one of the latest manifestations of the Oneness phenomenon: the Sacred Chambers. As I mentioned in the last chapter, one of my visits to the Sacred Chambers allowed me, experientially, to have a profound healing in regard to my mother. I was able to do that because the Sacred Chambers hold the space for people to have a direct sensory experience of their personal Divine in action, without any intermediary. We call that experience *grace*.

Grace, to me, is the unexpected gift that swoops in, delivering a shift in consciousness or manifestation that my own little ego-mind could not possibly have engineered on its own. Grace brings me to my knees in gratitude. It lets me intimately connect with the mystery that is life. It allows me to touch The Presence that infuses all life with its existence. When grace envelops me, I feel that I'm being held in the sacred embrace of my inner Divine.

Again, it doesn't matter what you call it or believe it to be; there is a universal *something* going on that we don't understand. This one something informs art, music, and science. It makes birds fly south for the winter, flowers bloom, sperm and eggs grow into humans, and the planets orbit. It heals the sick and brings hope to the despairing. To experience this great mystery so intimately is to feel humility and intense joy. As you continue to read in this book the many stories of rapid transformation and healing, you'll hear the word *grace* spoken over and over in amazed appreciation and joy.

Whose heart doesn't yearn for this ecstasy? Our minds delude us into thinking we can create this kind of joy if we are clever enough to win the game of life. But actually, grace is our birthright and it brings a bliss and perfection to life that money can't buy. We just need to open to it, to allow grace to express itself. The allowing starts by looking within to see what blocks our awareness of our authentic essence and innate connection to grace. The bulk of blockage lies in the unconscious, and we need big help to move it. The grace of Deeksha, Oneness courses, and Sacred Chambers can provide this help. Rev. Dr. Michael explains:

> In the Sacred Chambers, we contemplate 15 points to help bring us closer to the Divine. For instance, the biggest obstacle to intimacy with God is the bag of hurts we all carry around. The only way to shed those hurts and to forgive those who have hurt us is to fully experience the pain.
>
> Most of our pain is in the unconscious. You can't go looking for it. The Divine will bring it into our awareness and give us the grace to face it, not

run away from it. Fear, for example, is just the emotion of running away from something unpleasant. The answer is to stop running, turn around, and face it. Then there is no more fear. But we can't stop running. We'll try to do that but it requires grace. All these Oneness teachings are asking us to simply see this. Simply see that there is fear and ask for Divine grace. Simply see that there is hurt, and ask for Divine grace. See that you've hurt other people. Seeking forgiveness is to put yourself in their place and feel the pain you have caused them. That, too, is a gift of Divine grace that enables you to be the other person and feel what he or she is feeling.

A Dynamic Heart Connection

The way grace shows up for individuals will be as unique as their relationship to their Divine within. With time, and after doing a number of Oneness processes, my relationship with my personal Divine has evolved. In fact, I have a small team of Divine beings with me now. Generally, each of these sacred aspects of the Divine is like having a very dear, close friend and partner who always loves me unconditionally, helps me grow spiritually and stay healthy, consoles me when I'm sad, delights me with abundant miracles, and offers constant guidance.

For some people, their personal Divine may have a beloved parental quality, like a cherished mother or father, or another type of quality such as a loving brother or sister, or a wise, benevolent teacher. Personal Divines might look like animals, well-known religious figures, ascended masters, angelic beings, avatars, or aspects of nature, or they may appear like your next-door neighbor.

Our relationship with our personal Divine is a dynamic, unfolding connection. As with any other relationship, it isn't fixed, but evolves over time. Through grace and many experiences of receiving its healing, guidance, and love, our relationship moves from being based on a concept to being felt as a living heart connection and known through the senses. But often, the relationships we've had with our parents and others can make it hard for our heart to open up to a personal Divine.

Accessing this deep place in your heart requires vulnerability. Most of us have spent years developing armor to cover up hurts and protect vulnerability. The Oneness courses, so filled with grace, offer many opportunities to find the unique key that opens the door to your Divine. It may take intention and courage to unlock that door, but when it does open, we find the Divine fully ready to swoop in. Then we are returned to a state we once knew, perhaps only in the first hours of our newborn life; we are returned to a deep knowingness that we are unconditionally loved and protected by a highly intelligent, universal Presence.

Susan Leigh Babcock, an Awakened, Advanced Oneness Trainer, has a lovely description of her relationship with her Divine now. She says,

The most extraordinary shift I've experienced
since the Oneness Blessing found me—because

the Oneness Blessing always finds us, not the other way around!—is the active presence of the Divine spirit in my everyday life. I talk with my Divine source; my Divine source guides me and gives freely to me. I've turned over the future to my Divine source, and I dwell in the present of my Divine source.

If you haven't experienced it, I can't describe it in a way that you'd "get it" or even believe me. So trust me when I say this (or not): it is a total game-changer in the way life is lived and experienced. Many times it is close to ecstasy. Other times it's as if life is happening so easily; that it's the most natural thing in the world. Except that before, it wasn't.

A Practical Relationship

What Susan describes is the practical way that our Divine within (or whatever name we call it) shows up so extraordinarily in ordinary, everyday life. Rev. Mahaal Ajallahb, an Awakened Oneness Trainer, Oneness Meditator, and Sacred Chambers Facilitator, also has a practical approach in his relationship to his Divine. He grew up in Jamaica, the child of two ministers, and wanted a different kind of relationship with God than the one that was expected of him:

I remember growing up as a child, and hearing all the messages in church. I used to take notice of things that were spoken of experiencing God. I always wondered, "Why do I have to wait until I go to heaven?" It always annoyed me when I heard of the "still, small voice" within me. Why does God have to speak in this still, small voice? Why is it that you can hardly hear this voice? I wasn't having any of that! I wanted a practical, clear experience with God.

When Rev. Mahaal moved to the United States, he brought with him a passionate intention for a practical, everyday experience with God. His passion was met with a powerful response of grace:

I got up in a rage one morning. I said to God, "You better come talk to me and tell me what's up!" I knew nothing about the Oneness Phenomenon then, but I was talking to people about oneness. I went back to bed and in the middle of the day, the roof of the house opened up!

I looked down at this body lying on the bed (myself). I had what people call a near-death experience, but I call it a near-life experience. I ended up in a place where I saw deceased people who were still living the same lives they had been living when they had a body. I visited some other places, and then came back to my house, to the open roof, and sat next to my body for a little while. Then, boom, I was back in my body. From that day onward, I was more determined to have a practical life experience with God, walking and talking with God, whatever that is, however that works; I said, "God, YOU show me."

The Oneness Blessing found Rev. Mahaal through his partner, Elizabeth. He says he went kicking and screaming, but quickly realized his affinity for Oneness and its founders, Sri Amma and Sri Bhagavan:

I used to call my spiritual guides "Cosmic Dudes" without knowing who they were...but when I first heard Bhagavan talking, I was in heaven. I recognized him as a Cosmic Dude, and I thought, "Finally, a physical being who gets this about walking and talking with God."

For us to rise in consciousness, it literally takes the Divine to be alive in us. It also takes the Divine to walk and talk with us...so it can help us. In the process of healing, transcending, and rising in consciousness, the Divine is taking this step for human beings to grow, and grow in a practical way.

What I discovered for myself is that my Divine is available for every single ordinary activity of daily life. That is the practicality that Rev. Mahaal is talking about, and that's why awakening is no longer just for monks in secluded monasteries or those who have studied the ancient texts for 50 years.

Awakening is for real life, and it is a shift in awareness that happens to make ordinary life quite extraordinary. Whether I need help with a parking space, healing a serious illness, or paying the rent, I *know* my inner Divine is available to help me. This is the knowing that is filling that aching hole of loneliness, searching, and craving within. In the next chapters, it will become clear just how practical this cosmic *something* within can be.

CONTEMPLATION

1. Do you struggle with a belief in a universal higher power that is there for you, personally, all the time?

2. What concepts about God, if any, did you inherit from parents, ancestors, or the religion of your upbringing?

3. What kind of personal Divine or higher force would you like to have? What would you call it?

CHAPTER 5

The Role of Ancestors

The Awakened One has a bird's eye view of everything.

—Sri Bhagavan

Weekly Teachings, Week 194: June 1–7, 2014

Oneness University teaches that there are three primary causes for problems in our life: Relationships, karma, and the need for ancestor liberation. Similar to our relationships with our personal Divine, our family, and all who help to define our human existence, so much of our relationship to our ancestors often lies unexplored, buried deep in unconsciousness. This unconsciousness has its price, for unresolved problems of our ancestors that are preventing their souls from fully returning to the Light can hinder our own happiness. The Oneness Blessing phenomenon offers important processes that bring our ancestors into conscious awareness and give us the opportunity to ask grace for their liberation.

We've discussed the importance of healing relationships because the quality of our relationships determines the quality of life we have. We are nothing without our relationships. If we have good relationships, we have a good life. If our relationships are contentious, our life is full of battles.

Through the effect of our thoughts, the words we speak, and the actions we take, we generate karma. What we put out in the world comes back to us, many times over. This is a fundamental, spiritual law of the universe, and it includes all the good things we think, say, and do, as well as the things that do harm to others. What most of us aren't aware of is that we inherit ancestral karma too; what our ancestors have thought, said, and done comes back to us. Every country has karma, as well, which also affects us via the actions of ancestors. In the United States, many of us became citizens as a result of our ancestors leaving their homes, sometimes in order to escape poverty or persecution. Many came through force, as slaves. As a result, people lost much of their deep cultural traditions and history. Vocal or written records of family trees were buried in the chaos of creating new lives. Some records and stories were purposefully not passed down because the memories were too painful to speak of. Sadly, in many cases, cultural reverence for ancestors was lost to the pressing imperatives of survival in a new land.

For most of my life, I was quite unaware of the huge ancestral lineage carried in every cell of my being. Certainly, I'd been informed about genetic tendencies for hair and skin color, physical build, temperament, and certain diseases, but the profundity of my ancestors' influence on my happiness never sank in until I started working as an energy healer. Handed down from generation to generation in our genes and our energy field are the records of countless lives filled with trauma, pain, and joy. Have you considered that beliefs about money, success, health, work, and love are passed down? Or that unfinished business between family members and generations is passed down?

In working as a shamanic practitioner, through training and experiences, I've had visions of clients' past lives that also impact karma and current life. With clairvoyant sight, I see beliefs and conditioned patterns from parents and ancestral lineages embedded in the chakras and aura, and can see when soul parts of deceased relatives have not yet gone to the Light due to unresolved trauma or attachments at death. So I naturally resonate strongly with the Oneness teachings about ancestor liberation. From an energetic standpoint, it totally makes sense. Many ancient teachings all over the world speak of the importance of helping our relatives move to higher realms after death. Similar to the concepts of Heaven and Hell in the Bible, the ancient Hindu Scripture describes how souls can go through a series of lower realms (Hell) and a series of higher realms (Heaven) in order to reach the highest realm where souls will fully merge with the Light.

Even with my training and experience, when it came to embracing the potential magnitude of my ancestors' influence on so many aspects of my being, it took a number of Oneness courses and Divine grace to fully wake me up. It can be overwhelming and humbling to see how many factors affect our happiness. It's clear that we need the infinite power of grace to step in. Oneness University has brought forward ancient wisdom and provides processes to liberate our ancestors whose spirits have become trapped in different realms after death. Not only does their liberation free our ancestors for ultimate union with All That Is, but it also liberates us from certain problems and patterns we grapple with in our lives.

In Oneness, we honor our ancestors by asking our Divine (or whatever name you give that Higher Intelligence) to liberate them. Because these processes are so uniquely personal, you will have to have your own experiences to fully comprehend the impact of ancestors on your life. But if you find yourself with recurring problems affecting prosperity, health, relationships, success, and happiness, your ancestors may very well need liberating, and you will need the help of grace. We can't do it on our own, from the level of the mind.

A Story of Ancestor Liberation

Susan Leigh Babcock, an Awakened Advanced Oneness Trainer, received a powerful Sacred Chambers gift of grace that liberated her ancestors and healed a painful issue involving her own lack of self-acceptance. At the time, she was doing her work to recognize, honor, and heal her ancestors through Oneness processes and awareness. At the same time, with wonderful synchronicity, her sister was doing extensive research to construct their family tree. Additionally, with the bonus of having had chroniclers on each side of the family, Susan had a bevy of names, locations, and facts about her ancestors.

Going into the Sacred Chambers, all this information helped Susan understand some of the themes in her lineage, including those playing out in her own life. In her words,

Our New England settlers were a touch nomadic. Always on the move for better opportunities and lives, they migrated from Connecticut and Massachusetts to southern Vermont for the abundance of free farmland. Finding it too rocky to till, though, they crossed the border into New York State a few years later. I myself have moved a lot in my adult life, after a very stable childhood mostly in one place. I've always wondered why I've been driven to move so much!

Prior to coming to America, our British Isles ancestors, from both sides of the family, were either estate owners or servants. We had the upstairs branches and we had the downstairs branches. One couple, which I believe were great-great-grandparents, migrated here from the British Isles with nine children. On the way over, the father died on the ship. When the mother arrived, unskilled and unemployable, she had no way to take care of her children, so she indentured them. One of them was my great-great-grandfather. He was sold into a severe apprenticeship, with brutal work conditions and physical punishment. The effect on his adult life, late-in-life marriage, and offspring was devastating.

Susan took this knowledge, the day of the visit, into the first of three rooms that comprise the Sacred Chambers. The first chamber is for contemplation. Often visitors immediately begin to have insights from the powerful flow of grace there. Sure enough, in the first chamber, Susan received a significant awareness about a personal pattern that related to her ancestral history:

In the first of the Sacred Chambers I was shown a truth about my ancestors and myself. As I reviewed my life, my habits, and my desires, I realized I wasn't going to go very far if I didn't tackle the issue of self-acceptance. I seemed always to vacillate between seeing that I was pretty great and lucky and feeling like the black sheep of my family and a loser, of all things. These are feelings that, were I to share them, most people who know me would sputter over how ridiculous that sounds. But our feelings about ourselves rarely mirror any external reality. In fact, success can be a rabid effort to stave off feelings of worthlessness.

With this realization of the need to examine her lack of self-acceptance, she saw a Divine plan in that Sacred Chambers visit:

I had my mission decided before even arriving. Once I expressed it to myself, I was astonished to see, behind my closed eyes, a large crowd of ancestors. I'd seen them many times before in my visions during processes in which we called them in. This day, they were straining against a rope like you see at theaters and disco lines. "Let us go into the Second Chamber with you!" they cried. "Please! Please! Take us in there with you."

I realized that challenges I thought I was uniquely facing because of my own psychology or life's events were preceded and superseded. Here was an entire lineage of lack of self-acceptance. Beyond that, I was given to see that it played out on both sides of an insidious fence. On the one side were the land and estate owners who employed and sometimes victimized the servants and workers. These Lords of the Manor were, however, painfully aware of how they were afflicting these downstairs or outdoors classes. They were helpless to buck the societal norm, though, and continued their exploitation of the others, even while being acutely aware of and suffering for it internally.

The other side of the fence was the servants and workers. They were circumstantially abused and exploited. But they were equally afflicted with the realization that their Lords and employers were stuck in their world, and they themselves were simply on the wrong floor of the castle. They couldn't even feel self-righteously vengeful. Though they were hurt, the avenue of blame and retribution wasn't even open to them. With the clear-eyed recognition of their actual roles, with this seeing, downstairs suffered twice and upstairs suffered where most didn't.

Then Susan realized that, similar to her relatives, she also was stuck within a system:

As this unfolded behind my closed eyes like a historical costume drama, I realized that I was afflicted with the same painful awareness—painful because, in spite of seeing reality, I was stuck inside a system. The hurt and anger went out to this system rather than its participants because neither side wanted to vilify, condescend to, or blame the other.

Both classes blamed themselves. This was the root of my own lack of self-acceptance. I couldn't accept the times I was "made" by the system or another person to be an agent of oppression. And I couldn't accept that I was probably at fault for the suffering in my life. I often saw that suffering as circumstantial and blamed other people only uneasily, having enough insight, empathy, and understanding to thwart the perverse yet tempting pleasure of "the blame game."

Because of her visions and insights, Susan took the presence of her ancestors into the second Sacred Chamber, where visitors are able to ask their personal Divine for healing:

So we all went into the second chamber together. The ancestors weren't there physically with me, of course. But I still felt them coming in with me. I asked—we all asked—simply, for self-acceptance.

And in the third chamber, self-acceptance was given, just as simply.

With this huge blessing of healing, the way Susan feels about herself now is quite different:

What's different? Well, can you imagine accepting everything about yourself? All the parts of your body, all the aspects of your personality, all the mistakes you'd made, all the people you'd hurt, all the suffering life had brought to you and that had brought you to your knees? Can you imagine accepting that without judging yourself as a bad person, as less-than, as the black sheep?

That is what Oneness calls Liberation—in this case, Liberation from non-acceptance. Mind you, I still have parts that don't like being seen by me, and I still do my damnedest to hide those parts from others. And why not? But these parts are no longer cast out as the not-me. As I see that I am the sum of all these parts, I see these parts in others with much more compassion and love. I am the same as they are! They are no more or less than I am. We are all gloriously human. The foibles now seem endearing, the way we laugh at children when they make mistakes or fall down. They're children! We're human!

And my ancestors? They are liberated! They haven't shown up at the ropes since then. They are my friends; they help me and look over me, and they are happy. How do I know? I can't tell you. I can just say that I do.

Yes, sometimes you just know what you know! Other signs that might indicate ancestors have gone to a higher realm are that your body feels lighter, or you might have a vision that reveals it. Oneness University suggests that you ask your personal Divine to give you proof that your ancestors have been liberated.

Resources for Ancestor Liberation

An amazing thing about the Oneness Phenomenon is that resources for connecting with spiritual help are available throughout the world, both online and in person. One of the most recent gifts of the Oneness phenomenon is the Sacred Chambers. These chambers are located in many countries now, around the world, and if you can't attend Oneness University, where grace is extraordinarily strong and processes for ancestors are offered, you can visit a Sacred Chambers to pray for the liberation of your ancestors. Some Sacred Chambers actually specialize in liberation of the ancestors. Please see the Resources section of this book for Websites where you can discover the locations of these chambers and what they specialize in.

You can also take courses from Advanced Oneness Trainers who are certified to facilitate the Ancestor Liberation Process. Many of the Advanced Trainers who've contributed to this book are now offering these courses, as are trainers all over the world. I personally have taken an online Ancestor Liberation Process from Rev. Dr. Michael Milner, which was very profound, and I have also gone to Sacred Chambers (locally as well as to a Chambers that specializes in karma clearing) to ask my Divine for ancestor liberation. You can find out more information by looking at the Resources section.

CONTEMPLATION

1. What problems may be recurring in your life, despite your best efforts to "fix" them?

2. Are your relationships all in good standing, even the ones with deceased relatives? Are you harboring any grudges or were any of your relatives harboring any when they died? Are there any relatives whose death you haven't made peace with?

3. Are there any relatives who have visited you in dreams or visions? If so, did they convey a message or mood?

4. How far back can you trace your family tree? Can you identify any generational beliefs, values, sayings, or themes that you've adopted from ancestors or perhaps rebelled against?

CHAPTER 6

Abundance and Prosperity

The Awakened One has no problem with wealth—
for wealth is not the problem.

The unawakened one has a problem with wealth—
for the sense of possession is the problem.

—Sri Bhagavan

Weekly Teachings, Week 56: October 9–15, 2011

Many books have been written about the keys to having abundance and prosperity. I probably have read most of them, or at least they've sat on my bookshelf for a time before I gave them away in discouragement. I've obsessed about money, studied numerous strategies to try and make more of it, meditated on it, and panicked about its apparent lack. I know I'm not alone. Fear of not having enough of it is a biggie for many of us. Whether we have lots of it or little of it, an obsession with money can take center stage in our lives.

When the Oneness Phenomenon entered my life, I was feeling a lot of scarcity and depression regarding money. I had been working as a realtor to supplement my healing practice (which was part-time at that point), and the housing market in the United States had been spiraling downward. Every time I did a market analysis for someone's home and had to report how the value had plunged, I felt the way an oncologist might feel when conveying a cancer diagnosis. Selling real estate became a nightmare of lack and limitation; none of my listings were selling, the sellers were hostile, the buyers vanished, and I was anxious and paralyzed. The joy I had felt early in my career by helping people with such a significant part of their lives was gone. I discovered that fear of losing money brings out the worst in everyone, including myself. After some time, I sold my townhouse that I could no longer afford, rented a less expensive apartment in a new neighborhood, and hung up my real estate license.

I finally admitted to myself that I hadn't been enjoying real estate sales for quite a while, well before the recession hit. I wasn't thriving and felt little motivation or purpose. In retrospect, I saw that I could have left the profession earlier, but I'd been afraid. I didn't believe I would earn an adequate income doing anything else. Without the recession, I may have kept half-heartedly plugging away for years to come, and might have been quite miserable. But it turned out that this nation-wide crisis was my personal wake-up call, and I'm grateful for that bonk on the head, as painful as it was to go through.

After I gave up real estate sales, I tentatively committed myself to developing the healing practice that I'd kept on the sidelines, along with teaching, coaching, and a little blog writing for fun. I can say now, what a blessing! By huge grace, my work these days is immensely gratifying and flows from the heart. I'm also much happier living in a different location. But I can't pretend that I knew this is how things would turn out; I was depressed, moody, and fearful during much of the transition. On top of it, I was in the midst of the breakup of a six-year relationship as well. I felt as though my life was completely falling apart.

True Abundance

In the center of all the anxiety-provoking uncertainty and change, Deeksha and Oneness courses supported me in undergoing a lot of inner shifts that gradually began ushering tremendous joy into my life. As I started to awaken to a new, closer relationship with my inner Divine, a different sense of security was emerging from the wreckage. Faith in a greater plan kept me going, for there was much evidence of a sacred hand bringing many new people and events to me, all of which brought a huge amount of inner abundance and gratitude into my life.

Even though money was not yet showing up, a brand new and quite magical experience of true prosperity began to take root. Advanced Oneness trainer and Oneness Meditator Catherine Scherwenka describes this shift so well:

> In the past when I heard the words "abundance" and "prosperity," it was so conditioned to be about money. But now it's so much bigger than that. It has really expanded. It's a paradigm shift from material wealth to inner wealth, where your inner world is prosperous and abundant.
>
> Oneness has given so much abundance and prosperity to us on many levels. Our relationships get healed and they become abundant. Our internal world gets more and more clear, and becomes abundant with Divine grace. Your life just feels more prosperous on a day-to-day basis the more Divine grace is running your life. That's been my experience. There's a teaching that says your external world is a reflection of your inner world. When our lives are filled with so much grace, it's abundant in all aspects.

Factors that Limit Prosperity

The external world reflects the inner world because the beliefs we hold dear create our experience of life. Those beliefs were instilled in us through our families, schools, and society. Financial prosperity is available for everybody, but one reason that some people have more and some have less is because of the mind's belief system. Our beliefs can cause us to perceive life through the lens of lack. There's no reality to that lack. The reality is that the universe is exceedingly abundant, and every single one of us has inherited a potential for abundance. Whether we manifest that abundance or not depends not only on our beliefs and perceptions, but also on other factors such as our relationships, karma, and ancestors. As mentioned in Chapter 3, on healing relationships, Oneness teaches that our relationship with our fathers and mothers greatly affects our prosperity. It's important to work on healing those relationships first. We can also seek from our personal Divine (or whatever you call that universal creative intelligence) the liberation of our ancestors and the release of karma.

If you've done or are doing the work to heal the relationships with parents, karma, and ancestors, and are still experiencing prosperity difficulties, then it takes some courage and honesty to take a deeper look within and examine limiting beliefs, perceptions, and emotions about money. Money is a very charged issue and most of us have lots of baggage to sort through in this regard. Oneness processes are available to help with this endeavor. What we find, as we deeply examine our beliefs and fears, is that we need the help of grace to free ourselves of all the limitations and resistance affecting our prosperity.

Oneness teachings on abundance and prosperity generally concern two different arenas. One area of focus is our inner world. The second area of focus concerns the outer world and our actions in it. The inner world and our awakening to the Divine within is where we begin, because once that relationship to our personal Divine deepens, and we are following its lead, we have a limitless and authentic navigation system for action in the outer world. As we become conscious of our beliefs, perceptions, and emotions, calling on grace for help, then the outside world begins to reflect shifts in the inner world. We still have our part to do in the outer world, of course, and Oneness courses can provide guidance on understanding what is ours to do.

Wealth Consciousness

The more aware I've become of the beliefs and the emotional charges I carry related to prosperity, the more I've been able to see how constricted my consciousness has been for most of my life. The consciousness of lack and limitation is tight, joyless, and narrow. The consciousness of abundance and wealth is just the opposite. Abundance is spacious, gratitude-filled, and flowing. Having a consciousness of wealth includes seeing all the natural abundance of our life. We see that our wealth includes all the richness of our relationships, the exquisite blessings of grace, and the huge capacity for creativity and growth we come by naturally. Wealth consciousness is a consciousness of gratitude and appreciation for all that we have, including our Divine within.

After 20 years of dutifully reciting prosperity affirmations and efforts to create positive thinking through many different modalities, I still was not demonstrating consistent success in manifesting a lot of money. I would see myself slipping in and out of positive thinking and I struggled with self-esteem and feelings of frustration about why making money was such a challenge.

When I started taking Oneness courses—and, most especially, after awakening—I was finally able to have a much deeper awareness of the limiting money programming that stifles joy, service, and creativity. I came to recognize the voice of programming, with its platitudes and fearful outlook. I saw that my unconscious programming is so deep and pervasive that I absolutely needed grace to intervene, for growth in consciousness requires the help of something far greater than the rigid, controlling mind. Once I saw this, and once the bond with my personal Divine deepened, I could ask for the grace of wealth consciousness and begin to see some results. I've been able to see the powerful impact of my deepening relationship with my personal Divine.

Jumping off the Proverbial Cliff

Suppose you are similar to the way I was when my own crisis hit: you yearn to create those dreams you've been harboring of a life overflowing with joy, love, and abundant prosperity, yet you're lacking in self-confidence and over-equipped with fear and possibly even resignation. You feel stuck. All you see and experience is lack. When your wake-up call for an inner paradigm shift comes, and the call to transform is greater than your fear of staying the same, how do you jump off that proverbial cliff?

For me, the secret ingredient was the grace of Deeksha. It all has to start with a change in consciousness, and

Deeksha is a fantastic catalyst for just that. Deeksha circles, where you can receive numerous Oneness Blessings, along with Oneness courses and events create a fantastic field of grace that supports transformation.

Debra Apsara, an Awakened Advanced Oneness Trainer and Sacred Chambers Facilitator, describes how her first Deeksha launched a huge shift in consciousness:

> Oneness has basically changed my life. I would not be where I am right now without Sri Amma and Sri Bhagavan and Oneness. I spent much of my life suffering like you wouldn't believe and was stuck because I didn't know I was stuck. I actually had no way out because I didn't know there was anything wrong. I spent much of my life living in a state of suffering and I thought that was normal.
>
> What happened was I got sick, because that's what happens to bodies when you are suffering— the suffering spills over into the physical. My whole escape throughout life was to keep busy. My mom always kept busy and everyone kept busy in my home. I never took any moment to reflect on anything. I didn't know how to reflect. I wasn't spiritual and had no background or education in spirituality.
>
> As I hit that brick wall of illness, I had no choice but to stop and see, and what I saw was very scary. I saw that I wasn't happy. Then I got my first

Deeksha in January 2007, and it changed my life completely. I'll never forget that first one. My whole life, as I knew it, gradually began to fall apart over a period of two years. After two years, every single thing I knew to be me was gone. It was like a birthing took place, and it felt like I came out of a coma. I came out of being under the influence of what I now know is the mind; being totally controlled by programs and things that happened in my life. I finally saw that there actually is a natural state of joy in human beings in which there is no suffering, and there is just having pure, beautiful experiences that are meant to help you grow. I started seeing beauty in life where before I only felt negativity.

Deeksha can spark an avalanche of change in our whole view of life, as it did for Debra, or it can catalyze a slower, progressive series of shifts. Each of us has a unique path, but what is common to us all is that the change starts on the inside with increased self-awareness of our perceptions, patterns, and conditioning. With tremendous gratitude, we begin to see the inherent beauty, joy, and abundance that is life.

A New Navigation System

Deeksha can help in elevating the inner voice, the sacred voice of wholeness, making it loud enough to hear the guidance needed to take that next step on the journey of transformation. That's how we often get there, one insight or experience at a time, as we move from negativity and inner scarcity to inner *and* outer abundance. We come to rely on our inner guidance for every single matter in our life and the very unfolding of that life. That's the practical application and infinite possibility that change in consciousness offers.

Consider the words of Awakened Oneness Trainer, Oneness Meditator, and Sacred Chambers Facilitator Rev. Mahaal Ajallahb:

> Now just imagine you've been given a business, and someone who cares for you highly and deeply says, "I have some gifts for you, and some of those gifts I'm going to give you are the best advisors, the best board, the best banker, and all the best people from around the world at your disposal...and by the way, I have them in different time zones, so any time of the day, you can pick up the phone and get to them."
>
> What do you think you would do? You would be ecstatic that someone would care for you in that way, to make sure all the T's are crossed and all the I's are dotted so you have full support in every aspect of the business you're pursuing. Talking about practicality—this is the practicality that God is giving us, walking and talking with us!

If the idea of having a "God" doesn't work for you, just substitute whatever word resonates with you. Whether it's a word like Universe, Spirit, higher consciousness, Source, a totem animal, Buddha, your intuition, your Higher Self, or your soul, there is something powerful that can be accessed from the stillness within. There is something beyond the limited, conflicted, and conditioned mind; something that guides, comforts, heals, loves, and leads the way.

Before awakening, we are running on the self-will generated by the mind. The mind is always trying to get something, to acquire what we think we need to survive. It's a struggle to hear the inner voice amidst all the conflict generated by the mind. When the mind is dominating, we can only operate from the belief systems of the mind. Your thoughts, choices, and strategies will be subject to the collective unconscious and ancestral lineages that shape your thinking. But after awakening, when we are able to surrender to a higher consciousness to light the way, our relationship with the mind strongly shifts, which is why Oneness teachings say that awakening is being de-clutched from the mind. As Rev. Mahaal explains about the different relationship we have with the mind after awakening,

> You're acting in such a manner that you're not depending on the mind, but you're using the mind. When you are walking and talking with the Divine, the mind is still large, but the mind is not in charge. You are using the mind, instead of the mind being large and in charge and using you. You

start to have the experience of how to constructive-
ly use this tool called the mind, instead of it using
you.

When you awaken, your consciousness becomes an
unfolding of oneness consciousness. Therein lies the abundance, the connection to all that is, for life is exceedingly
abundant in nature. The infinitely creative power of consciousness is the truth of reality. From the consciousness
of reality, rather than from the conditioning of limitation,
unfolds all that you need.

A Prosperity Miracle

Debra Apsara has an outrageously swift prosperity miracle to share. It perfectly illustrates the infinitely, creative
power of a sacred Higher Intelligence and the way that a
deep connection to this sacred consciousness brings us
everything that we authentically desire:

> I was in the Sacred Chambers praying, and I
> needed to pay my rent. I told my Divine how much
> money I needed, and that the rent was due about a
> week later. I had been applying for so many nurs-
> ing positions, and no one was getting back to me,
> so I was pretty desperate and said to my Divine,
> "You've got to do something! I need the money, but,
> truthfully, I really don't want to work."

As I was praying, I heard the phone ringing. I answered it, and the woman on the phone said, "I booked your airplane ticket; here's your confirmation number." I had no idea what she was talking about, so she switched me over to a recruiter who explained a few things to me. I was to travel for two days and come back on the third day. The plane was leaving the next morning for San Jose, California, and I still had only minimal details about what I'd be doing. I just said to myself, "Okay, what the heck. I'll do it."

When I landed in San Jose, I checked in to the hotel where they'd booked me and was then sent to a large meeting room. I went through a whole signing-in process with a lot of paperwork, which I'd filled out in advance, and was told at the end that I'd be sharing a room with someone. I immediately said that I didn't want to share a room, but they said that everyone does that. So I reluctantly agreed. Then, to my surprise, I was handed a $100 bill because my paperwork had been filled out. They couldn't tell me what was happening after that, but said, "Come to the lobby tomorrow morning at 5:45 a.m., and you'll be picked up by a bus." When I went to the hotel room after that, I found out that I didn't have a roommate after all. No one was there. So I got the room alone!

The next morning, I was picked up by the bus and taken to a place where I would sit in a room all day long. It turned out to be an orientation, not to work, but to perhaps work in the future. It was called an induction. If a hospital in California were to have a strike, I might be called to fill in for other nurses. So I sat there all day, and they paid for my meals. I didn't do anything. I stayed over night and they flew me home the next day. So I never worked while I was there. I had never heard of anything like that in my whole career as a nurse.

When I was leaving that day, they gave me $1,150. With the $100 in cash, that came to $1,250. I had $50 at home, and my rent is $1,300. So I was able to pay the rent and never had to work, which is what I'd asked for from my Divine. We have a very good connection!

Inner Prosperity

Perhaps money is not a problem for you at all, or you are already successful in business. But even with plenty of money, you still feel unhappy or that something is missing; you're feeling empty inside because that connection to something greater isn't fully realized. Again, this is a consciousness issue. It's that illusion of separation. It's the false belief that we are separate from the inherent, great abundance of life and that we have to create abundance ourselves, for ourselves, with the sheer force of our will. This consciousness of lack is woven into our conditioning and has been re-created in the outer world by our beliefs, generation after generation. There are many people on this planet who are monetarily rich, but who do not have abundance consciousness. Awakening is the door through which we enter the higher consciousness of abundance and true prosperity. As Rev. Mahaal Ajallahb wisely notes,

For you to truly enjoy your wealth and see it as a gift, you have to be prosperous in your inner world. That prosperity is having God walk and talk with you, where you are now being given the qualities of your Divine more and more in every moment, in every experience. After a while, there is no "your way" and "God's way." There is just one way; it is only experiencing life in the most magnificent way.

So now you become clear that having a bond and friendship with your Divine is prosperity. It is having an abundance of conscious living in practicality, and it becomes a way of life. Your consciousness rises every moment and it is permanently expanding. As such, when it comes to money, significance, thriving, and success, it is all part and parcel of your practical experience in all aspects of your life—not just money, but including money as well.

So now the relationship with abundance and prosperity has shifted. We have prosperity

consciousness. We have abundance consciousness. We have wealth consciousness. Money, like everything else, is a sacred process. So we love it, and we treat it well, like everything else. Now our identity is not tied up in the minutiae of the mind. The mind looks at life through the lens of conflict.

Oneness teachings strongly encourage us to pursue our material desires in the outer world—there is no reason to deny yourself wealth, cars, homes, nice clothes, or any of the material treasures of modern life. In fact, Oneness teaches that it's important to fulfill these desires. But what shifts after awakening is our relationship to these things. As Rev. Mahaal says,

When the car or the house, or whatever has been the symbol of prosperity before, is no longer the focus, then we enjoy those things more. I want a fabulous house, the best-made luxury car ever. I choose to be wealthy. When we see abundance and prosperity for what it is, we start to see life in a whole new way because we are experiencing life differently. Abundance is not just about money and toys. Because we have a shift in consciousness, we can experience money and toys differently because we are experiencing life differently.

Are you beginning to see the impact that a shift in our relationship to prosperity and abundance would have on life if everyone awakened? If that were to occur, and the accumulation of money, power, and security was no longer the focal point in living and working, the abundance that comes from our true unity with each other would be realized. There would be an end to this disastrous trajectory on which the world has been careening.

Oneness Consciousness

Lying at the root of all of the poverty, wars, and destruction of the natural world is the consciousness of separation and lack. With a consciousness of oneness, on the other hand, there is only the abundance of connection and the limitless creativity to discover, negotiate, and utilize resources better. With high levels of awakening, we come to experience that extreme poverty in Africa, for example, is our own inner poverty. We come to intrinsically know that the pollution of faraway oceans and waterways is the pollution of our own water. It becomes clear that the plundering of rain forests in South America is the defilement of the wildness within us. With high levels of awakening, oneness consciousness provides the paradigm shift we need to end the ceaseless greed, destruction, and suffering.

This is not naïve idealism. The practical application of awakening looks as ordinary as having awareness about the effect of littering. Recently, I was driving behind a beautiful luxury car, and saw the driver toss an empty water bottle out the window as he sped along the road. *Wow,* I thought to myself, *here is the effect of separation conscious-ness right in my face.* Despite all the education about and fines imposed for littering by the state of Illinois, someone is still doing it. So I sent him an intentional Deeksha for awakening.

These words are not meant to place blame on anyone, any business, or any institution for the choices made and actions taken, given the level of consciousness of those decision-makers. In truth, we are all only doing the best we can with the consciousness we have. We're all subject to conditioning, karma, and the power of unconscious beliefs that perpetuate the illusion of separation. But this is why we profoundly need grace in order to change.

Perhaps reading these words will help you to under-stand why the blessing of awakening is such a huge benefit to all life, everywhere. It is an enormous gift to the world when each individual awakens. The fact that awakening is sweeping the globe gives us all reason to believe in a mass transformation of consciousness that will solve the prob-lems we urgently grapple with today.

What does it look like when one individual awakens to abundance consciousness? Rev. Mahaal describes how one person abundantly blesses others after awakening:

> The decisions you make [after awakening], you make from an awareness of how it will affect oth-ers. It's this kind of practicality that comes with walking and talking with your God, that makes you relate to the world better. It's not that you be-come a snob or a saint who can't relate to the world.

It's that you relate to the world from a place of love, of peace, of grace, of happiness, and of joy. Then you come to find out how you have successful relationships, a successful business, and how you have a successful life. You walk the planet as a happy being, enjoying every step. You see the beauty of a particle of dust blowing in the wind. You're mowing the lawn and you see the beauty of that. You go to a movie, and see the beauty of that.

You continue, then, to make beneficial decisions that affect your life in every aspect involved, and the entire planet. When you do this, you naturally make decisions that benefit the environment, your relationships, and the concerns of other people who work with you or for you. You are able to conduct every aspect of your life without any separation from any other aspect of your life. So going to a movie is no different from being in the boardroom. Being in the boardroom is no different from being with your family. Being with your family is no different from flying on a plane with people whom you previously would have considered strangers. Every experience now becomes a deepening and expansion in your consciousness.

This is the practicality of living, of which we had no idea before. This is what life is about. It's only then that we talk about abundance and prosperity.

For a long time, we have not associated abundance and prosperity with a way of life.

As a way of life, abundance and prosperity embody the sweetness of a life lived within a consciousness of awakening to oneness. This doesn't mean we won't have feelings, or experience any pain. But our relationship to everything changes. No longer is our conflicted mind plagued with questions like, "Why am I here?" or "How can I discover my purpose in life?" We are *living* our purpose. In the following chapter, we will explore the meaning and practicality of living your purpose in a world that is in the grip of suffering, and at the same time, beginning to transform right under our feet—through grace.

CONTEMPLATION

1. What did your father teach you through words or example about making money and being successful? What family patterns related to money did he continue?

2. What did your mother teach you through words or example about money? About staying safe? About being loved?

3. How is your relationship with money?

4. Do you spend more time worrying about what's lacking in your life, or feeling grateful for what life has given you?

5. Do you use your mind or does your mind use you?

CHAPTER 7

Your Purpose in a Transforming World

The Awakened One flows with life.
The unawakened one struggles with life.
—Sri Bhagavan

Weekly Teachings, Week 118: December 16–22, 2012

Sri Bhagavan has said that the purpose of life is to live. Oneness Blessings and processes support us in moving toward living our life authentically, from a place of creativity, passion, self-awareness, connection, and contribution. When we go through the shift into awakening, we no longer need to wonder what our purpose is, for in being released from the clutches of our conflicted, doubting mind, we are simply living the unfolding of Higher Intelligence.

It becomes clear that our purpose is being fully alive, growing in consciousness, deepening our relationship with the Divine within, and doing our part in sacred collaboration with life in a way that benefits everyone. Our living is a continual process of growth. The greatest success comes when we are living authentically and experiencing gratitude for what life gives us. It all begins in the internal world of each individual. As each person transforms, so will the world.

In this chapter, I share with you the stories of four individuals whose lives changed profoundly by their involvement in the Oneness Blessing Phenomenon. As they deepened in their bond with their inner Divine, aided by the grace-filled catalysts of Deeksha and Oneness experiences, the revelation of renewed purpose occurred in unimaginable ways, showing a Divine orchestration behind it all. These people happen to be Oneness trainers, but becoming a trainer isn't required for the synchronistic progression of events in the way that each experienced. Quite the contrary; with grace, this can and will happen to anyone with a strong intention to connect with their heart's desire, to grow in consciousness, to bring good to others, and to awaken to the truth of their being. The Oneness phenomenon happens to provide some profound tools to support what amounts to a rapid paradigm shift for those who want it.

One day, back in the mid-1980s, before I even knew what I was asking for, I made a strong plea to my Divine to use me to help awaken humanity's consciousness. I had been observing what I saw as a deep, pervasive, spiritual famine in our country and was terribly disturbed by it. I passionately wanted to contribute to creating consciousness change somehow. I was working as a realtor, and wanted to work in another field, but I didn't have the slightest idea what else to do. Even though I had a longstanding (but closeted) passion for writing and had majored in English literature, I didn't have the confidence to write professionally. I investigated different masters degree programs in counseling, but none fully resonated. Because no other options presented themselves, I continued working in real estate for several more years, got married, and gave birth to my daughter.

My Divine clearly knew my repressed passion to write and heard my plea to help others, but it took a number of years and the completely unexpected and painful collapse of my marriage to set me on a new path. A series of events pushed me in the direction of becoming a massage therapist and then a shamanic healer. Shamanic healing was something I'd never heard of before (even though it is thousands of years old), so I didn't have a clue that I would love it the way I do. As it turned out, the skills it required of me came very naturally. What was most necessary was for my Divine to shove me, in a quite forceful way, beyond the limitations of my mind, which held me stuck in fear and passivity. Even working as a shamanic healer, helping clients shift and grow, I had many more years of my own suffering and struggle to go through until my life again changed dramatically, when I encountered the Oneness Blessing.

I tell you my story to emphasize two things: first, the power of passion, which is the sacred energy of the Divine within, to lead us into an expanded calling; second, the swiftness of transformation that can occur once Deeksha is received. What took me almost three decades of fear and doubt before I could move into greater peace and contribution is seen to occur in a few years or less in the Oneness Phenomenon.

I'm still amazed by the orchestration of Divine grace that brought me the opportunity to write a book about consciousness. Grace had to move mountains of stubborn resistance. If a miracle like this can happen to someone like me, it can happen to you too! Shifts are becoming even more rapid at the present time, due to the many thousands of people now awakening, who are raising the collective level of consciousness, making it easier for everyone to transform.

From Crisis to the Miraculous

The unfolding of authentic purpose can start, as it did for me, with some sort of crisis or crossroads that signals a need for change, pushing us in a new direction. Something bubbles up from within; a persistent call to expanded contribution and fulfillment. Oneness Trainer and Oneness Meditator, Catherine Scherwenka, shares her story of awakening to a new purpose in living that began amidst the powerful aftershocks of the traumatic event of 9/11:

I was a celebrity hair stylist in New York City before I found Oneness. I felt lost the whole time I was living in Manhattan. I didn't feel like I belonged. I had a lot of existential questioning about whether this was all there was to life. I was trying desperately to fill that void and those questions running around in my mind with external, material things.

The more I would gain in the external world, the emptier I would feel in the internal world. It wasn't making sense. I always felt like I was supposed to be doing something greater, and I was always drawn to helping humanity, but I would get so frustrated by the overwhelming enormity of helping starving children, or battered women, war, and conflict. So I would just freeze and give up; I would think, "What can little old me do?" I thought about becoming a lawyer or going into politics to try and help the state of the world, but I always got frustrated and gave up.

I ended up putting myself through New York University to get my degree. I hoped that by doing that, I would feel more comfortable in the world, receive more recognition, and have a sense of fitting in. But that, too, did absolutely nothing for me as far as helping me feel like I fit in. When there is pain inside, you can rearrange the furniture to try and make yourself feel better, but it's the same old furniture. Then, 9/11 hit New York City. It was obviously a huge wake-up call for New York City, the country, and the world. Our country had never before had to deal with fear to that magnitude. At that time, I was a business partner with another woman and we owned a very successful business. I was engaged to be married. I was going to have a fairy-tale wedding, have two kids, a dog, and a white picket fence, and really do my best to fit in to society. All the while, though, I was feeling emptier and emptier inside.

When 9/11 hit, it either brought people closer together or pulled them apart. In the case of my fiancé and me, it tore us apart. My fiancé lost about 25 of his good friends and I lost my college roommate in the devastation that was 9/11. It was horrific. With the shock, I realized that I just couldn't live the life I was leading anymore; I was giving up. I sold my half of the business to my partner, and decided to move to Montana and go back to school. Everyone thought I was insane. They couldn't understand how someone could give up all this wealth, prestige, and significance. I was walking away from all the things that supposedly make up the American dream. I didn't care. I needed to get reconnected to nature and to something bigger than myself.

My twin sister, meanwhile, had found Oneness. She wanted me to go to the 21-day course at Oneness University with her to become a Blessing Giver. Even though I wanted to go, and even though I could feel and experience the changes that were taking place inside of her, my skeptical mind had a grip on me. I was so full of fear and skepticism that I said no. When she came home from Oneness University, I could witness and feel even greater shifts in her. I then decided to go myself. I went with skepticism, judgment, lack of faith, and with no God in my life. But by the end of the 21-day course, I started having glimpses. All we need is a glimpse. We just need that little taste to believe that something greater is out there that can make our life become more magical.

I met the guides at Oneness University on the first day I arrived. It was so funny, because they thought I was my twin sister! The energy and presence they held planted a seed in my heart, and that became my purpose: I didn't want anything else except what they had. I wanted the energy, the joy, and the calmness that emanates from these remarkable beings. That became my drive and my purpose. I would do anything to get that, so I pretty much dedicated my life to Oneness after that. I did a lot of volunteering and lived at Oneness University for a long time.

My life has become more and more magical through it all. If I had known back then that my life would be what it is now, I wouldn't have believed it. It is miracle after miracle every moment of my life now. Oneness says that life is a miracle, and that has really become my reality. All those things I was striving for in New York are amazing and they create a beautiful being, but we shouldn't get stuck in thinking that's who we are. We define ourselves by all these personalities, from these diplomas and papers that give us credibility, but that's not what your heart is. It's amazing to have all those things in addition to your heart and your connection to your Higher Self.

Let Authenticity Be Your Guide

A life that is fully lived can't help but abundantly bless those it touches. The inherent nature of authenticity is abundance itself. Oneness teaches us how to strengthen our relationship with what is sacred to us and brings us joy. Deeksha catalyzes our alignment with this authentic, creative part of our being, and heightens self-awareness, so that we can manifest the joy, passion, and contribution our hearts long to share with the world.

Oneness Trainer and musician Tazdeen Rashid was one of my first Oneness teachers, along with another trainer whom he recently married, Biana Mavasheva. Similar to Catherine, Taz's connection to his purpose really took off after hitting a major turning point in his career. When I met Taz, he was leading Deeksha circles with Biana, teaching Oneness Awakening courses, and working a full-time corporate job. One day, he was unexpectedly let go from his job, and his life began to change dramatically. Here is Taz's story:

Around the middle of 2011, I was let go of from my corporate job. The timing was actually perfect because I was scheduled to go to India two weeks later, to attend a month-long course at Oneness University. I made plans to come back from India and start a home health job as an executive director with some other entrepreneurs, but when I got back from Oneness University, my whole body said, "No! This is not for you." So I declined that offer and began doing some random jobs. I had no idea what I was going to do. I was unemployed, but just began tinkering around, and that's when the magic really started. While at Oneness University, it had come to me in a powerful way that my Divine was my business partner and I had decided to trust that.

One little project after another emerged. I just kept saying yes to what showed up. Each little job led to another. I happened to attend a big yoga and music festival in California that year, and I had the thought that it would be very cool to have that same festival in the Midwest. Within three months,

I was working for that festival as the main organizer of their event in the Midwest. I was doing things for them that I'd never done before, like organizing vendors, but it all kind of worked with things I had envisioned before.

More opportunities like that began popping up, left and right. Between 2011 and now, 2014, it has come to a point where I am being hired by some of the largest yoga festivals to do music, which is my passion. I am making albums, making music, which is what I've always wanted to do. Along the way, I was being a DJ and also making music, such as playing percussion in a kirtan group, but I always thought I liked being the side guy, supporting other musicians because it was less responsibility and more fun. Now I've become the musician who is holding the energy. I'm putting CDs together with my original music and recording guitar and didgeridoo.

I now have relationships with international producers. I'm the musician and I'm also sitting in the producer seat with these other producers. I'll also be representing a large, eco-conscious organization, and we're in full swing creating that. All these things led from one thing to another in the most synchronous ways. Even though I started working with this organization in 2012, I had no idea that I'd been doing the kind of work I am now with their music division. It's all just amazing, and sticking with it is key. Effort is very important.

Oneness courses stress that we have work to do in our internal world as well as in the external world. The nature of our effort is quite different in each world. The inner-world work of transformation invites us to deepen our bond with whatever is sacred to us and to ask this sacred energy for help. We become aware of our programming and charges, and can do certain practices if we desire, which, along with Deeksha, raise *Kundalini*, the Sanskrit term for "life-force energy." Oneness calls all this "effortless effort" because it is passive and internally focused, as opposed to more active, externally focused *doing*.

The external world requires us to take physical action, to put forth conscious effort. When we awaken, we find that both internal and external arenas merge and flow with much grace and ease. In fact, the flow is so strong that it's quite difficult, perhaps impossible, to resist.

Oneness has valuable information to communicate about understanding our role in manifesting our desires. We come to see how deep our programming is and how much grace we need to succeed beyond programming's grip. The teachings are offered in beautiful and practical ways, but they're really meant to guide us as we move deeper into awakening. It is grace that actually allows us to experience the teachings in ways unique for each of us. When we awaken, this is very clear.

As we live an awakened life, more fully engaged in our purpose and filled with immense gratitude, we see that success flows. Taz explains more about the way Oneness has taught him to view growth and success:

Oneness teaches that strong intent, plus effort, plus grace, equals success and growth. I believe that even if the intention and effort is 1 or 2 percent, and the rest is grace, that small percentage on our part is extremely important. For us, in this human form, that effort is everything we know of in our little human minds, but the grace is so big we can't even imagine it. That grace is the Divine orchestration that's bringing everything together, and not just for me. It's beyond what we can comprehend. That's the living matrix. But we have to do our part, to our capacity. We have to turn the knobs; we can't just sit back and expect everything to happen.

When the Divine opens certain doors for us, it's up to us to walk through the doors and do the work. When someone invites me to do something, I look at it as my Divine inviting me to a certain project or situation. Then I look into it to see if it fits with my intention and mission in life right now. If it's a full-body yes, then I really go forward and make it happen.... This is how abundance is flowing through everything in my life now.

Exactly what we are doing doesn't matter as much as the reason we do it. When we are doing what we do in alignment with our inner guidance, and when we have clarity and honesty about the source of our desires, we will see that our process unfolds quite magically. Taz explains how important it is to fully embrace our authentic desires:

The whole mission of Oneness is for people to live their lives as authentically as possible. One of the biggest things I've learned through Oneness is not to hold any judgments about anything I want in life. Everything I want is perfectly fine, as long as it doesn't harm anyone. Whatever my desires are, I don't hold onto any feelings like, "This is bad," "I'm greedy," or "This is gluttonous." When I experience the things I really want, I feel so happy and blissful from a grounded and connected place. That happiness and bliss show me that those things are for me.

My vision is that I want to awaken people with music, dance, and creativity and allow them to see that they are creative, Divine beings. I created this vision in 2011, and it's even truer now; it's become reality. Now, a slightly new vision is emerging that involves traveling globally, doing music, and creating huge festivals that inspire, build, and actually improve a community. I've learned, though, to hold the vision and allow the universe to give it to me. The negative self-judgment is what blocks us from

129

fully receiving the invitations the Divine is trying to give us. When we clear our own personal judgments, we can really start receiving abundance.

Divine Orchestration

Kristin Panek was the third trainer in a powerful threesome of Oneness Trainers (along with Taz and Biana) who blessed me with the Deeksha Giver initiation course. Kristin also went through a major shift as she moved deeper into experiences with the Oneness phenomenon and awakening. She explains the perfect orchestration of events that ushered her toward become a Oneness trainer and then, more recently, to become a Sacred Chambers Facilitator:

I took my first Blessing Giver initiation course in Fiji. When I came back home, I felt somebody was pushing me from out there; something had shifted inside, and I felt an external push to go out and start teaching meditation classes. But I knew nothing about that! So I thought, "Well, this is weird," but I created a flyer and put it out at the yoga studio, and people showed up! The meditations started downloading through me and it worked out beautifully.

Then I was inspired to lead a couple's workshop with my husband, Frank, so we did a few of those and they were really powerful. Then I was inspired to teach meditations in the pitch dark, so I did some of those. Then I was inspired to teach yoga, so I did that. But all of these things seemed really disconnected, and I wondered why I was doing all these different things. Then in February 2010, Oneness University came out with the Oneness Awakening Course and I went for the teacher's certification training. I realized that everything I had been teaching came together in that course! I had been trained to teach the course before it was even offered!

So that was huge for me. Not only was it getting my work out in the world, but I was also beginning to trust my intuition and act on it in a way I had not been able to make myself do before. Since then, my journey has continually increased my trust in my intuition and my connection to the Divine.

Every time I think I am comfortable with where I am, then I'm presented with the next leap. Take the Sacred Chambers, for example: I was comfortable delivering Oneness Awakening courses and doing what I do, and then the opportunity to facilitate the Sacred Chambers came along. That was another leap of faith, as well as a learning experience. It changed everything about the way we do things here at our center. That's what Oneness has been doing; it's been leading me to places of *expansion, both in consciousness and in the way I move in the world.*

Expansion in Reach

Just as Kristin mentions, when consciousness expands, so does the way we move in the world. One by one, each awakened person having a consciousness of oneness naturally shines a light of expansiveness and freedom that helps others to shift in that direction. Awakening creates leaders who will be transforming the world for generations to come. The transformation starts with each individual, and as the stories of Catherine, Taz, and Kristin illustrate, their inner expansion and transformation naturally unfolds in the external world as having an increasingly greater impact and reach.

Angelika Schafer, an Awakened Oneness Trainer, Sacred Chambers Facilitator, musician, composer, and internationally recognized recording artist, has experienced that same expansion of her reach through Oneness, allowing her to step more fully into sharing her beautiful talents. Here is her story:

In the late summer of 2005 I was introduced to Deeksha. I started to offer my music at Deeksha seminars because I felt deeply inspired. Shortly after that, I traveled to Oneness University to become a Deeksha Giver. While there, I was invited to sing for a large group of people from all over the world during a Darshan with Sri Bhagavan. It was such a blessing.

Up until that time, I had been supporting my healing music ministry by doing other work, so I could do the music with a pure heart and without the pressure of needing to make money. But what happened after returning from Oneness University was surprising. Right away, literally the day after returning, I was invited to sing at a Ron Roth event in California by new friends who had heard me sing in India at that Darshan. Much to my surprise, for the very first time, my briefcase full of CDs totally sold out.

Then I was invited to sing at Oneness conferences all over the world, including an event in Taiwan with 3,000 people. It was amazing because gradually what happened was that I had no time to do the other jobs anymore and the music became a full-time work of love, which also provided a livelihood. The music I do was always for the Divine, this was clear from the beginning, but since I have received the grace of Deeksha, the music is definitely infused with that blessing power. It holds and transmits that vibration.

With the help of a friend and land partner, I was also able to gradually build the wilderness retreat on the property where we live, which now includes the Sacred Chambers.

Shortly after returning from my first trip to Oneness University, while working on my CD "Benediction" (I was recording it in the cabin in the woods where I live), I looked out the window one day and saw a rainbow. I love rainbows, and they are always an uplifting love message for me, so I stepped outside and took a picture with my digital camera. A few weeks later, when I finally transferred the newest pictures to my computer, I couldn't believe my eyes. There, next to the rainbow, was a big, silver heart in the sky, made of 3 orbs of light and a ray of light trailing down toward earth from this heart. It was such a deliberate message of love for me and truly a miracle. I get a chuckle out of other people trying to explain it! I am still deeply touched by this photo every time I see it.

I view everything in my life now as given by grace. I have undergone deep transformation, which is not always easy, but I wouldn't change a thing. I am very grateful for this phenomenon; grateful for Deeksha, and for Sri Amma and Sri Bhagavan, who brought Deeksha forward, for blessing my life in such profound ways.

CONTEMPLATION

Reflect on the timeline of events that make up your life. Do you see the footprints of a universal Higher Intelligence at work? With hindsight, do you see a purpose for each event happening the way it did?

CHAPTER 8

Relief from Cravings and Addictions

Freedom is not in the transformation of the "what is."
It is in witnessing the "what is."
—Sri Bhagavan

Weekly Teachings, Week 191: May 11–17, 2014

In a sense, we are all addicts; in our conditioning, we get attached to so many beliefs, habits, and concepts that come from the mind rather than reality. We acquire habitual responses, deeply entrenched in our programmed ways of relating to life, that cover up uncomfortable feelings we don't want to feel. Most of the time, we're reacting in the same old patterns. Because of our conditioning, and the mind's overpowering drive to predict, assess, and control, we miss all the side paths, the surprises, and the unpredictable essence of life's freedom that is only possible when we are living from the heart, not the mind.

Whether we term it *addiction, habit, pattern,* or *attachment,* it is a complex web of behavior and physiology that begins as an attempt to cope with fear, but limits our freedom to fully experience life. Most of the time, we're not even aware of this limitation and lack of freedom. The Oneness Blessing phenomenon is a catalyst for coming out of this mass slumber. It initiates an experiential rise in the freedom, infinite creativity, and expansiveness of our spirit, which has qualities quite the opposite of addictive, habitual response. We begin to see that we embody creative potential as part of our authentic nature. In awakening, we step into freedom from the bondage of the limiting, craving, and addictive mind.

Conditioning and Craving

Craving and addiction show up everywhere in our culture. We're bombarded with advertising that plants the seeds for conditioned craving at a very young age. Even 3-year-olds crave a certain doll or toy after seeing it on television, and pin all their hopes on Mom or Dad giving it to them for their birthday. Soon, birthdays comes to mean happiness because you get the toys you want. Ever see the sad face of a child who didn't get the toy he wanted?

How different is that conditioning from habitually craving a beer, a glass of wine, a cigarette, or some chocolate to take away the day's stress after work? Like children's toys on birthdays, these substances come to embody the illusory promise of happiness. Each time we go for a substance to relieve emotional discomfort, we risk losing touch with the underlying feelings of anger, fear, or sadness that can get covered up with the substance or activity we're using to escape. When we habitually stifle our feelings, they build up and block new insights, and can even lead to diseases and chronic physical problems. When the craving or addiction takes hold, we'll begin to feel stuck, like we're in a hopeless rut of inner conflict.

Oneness teaches us to fully experience our emotional charges by staying with the "what is," thereby moving through those charges into an authentic state of joy. In our authentic being, we *are* joy. We are free. We are creative. We have the thing that most humans want, which is to be happy. Until we are awakened, staying with the "what is" to fully experience our charges is hard to do. Getting Deeksha gives us a huge boost and catalyzes a liberation process from the mental conditioning that creates habits and addictions, even the habit of suppressing our feelings. Our conditioning is so incredibly thick and deep that it's hard to cut through its grip, let alone see it. It's woven into our brain's structure. But with the help of Deeksha, and most especially after awakening, it's a whole different ballgame.

After awakening, you might come home upset one day, but you know from experience that you can't escape your feelings by eating a chocolate bar. You're aware that your emotional discomfort will continue until you fully experience it. You remember you've got some chocolate in the house, but the chocolate doesn't rule you. You now have a choice whether or not to eat the chocolate; maybe you eat it because you really love the taste of it, or maybe you don't, but you can't avoid your feelings, whether you eat the chocolate or not.

It's frequently observed and experienced in Oneness circles that Deeksha and awakening offer a natural opportunity to find relief from one's addictions and cravings. Even before awakening, receiving Deeksha provides unique assistance to those who want to change some habitual ways of acting or thinking. How does this happen? Well, I talked with three Oneness trainers about this significant aspect of the Oneness phenomenon, and each offered a different angle.

Eat What You Want

Here's how Awakened Advanced Trainer and Oneness Meditator Catherine Scherwenka has experienced relief from her cravings through the Oneness Blessing phenomenon:

> In Oneness, one of the things that is very different from other traditions is that we are taught to fulfill our desires instead of renouncing them. Almost all other traditions say to renounce your desires, not fulfill them. In the beginning, this teaching was confusing to some people. But in

Oneness, we are taught that when you fully experience something, it will naturally fade away, whereas when you try to resist and renounce something, it only creates a bigger energy of wanting it.

This has completely been my experience. I was more of the renouncing type, where I would give things up. All in all, that's not good for me—I can't do that. The longer I was in Oneness, and the more I heard this teaching, I started saying, "Okay, I'm going to fulfill my desires. I'm going to let myself eat sugar and see if I die from eating too much sugar." In actuality, I ate enough of it, and what happened was that something shifted inside my brain and inside my body. All of a sudden, I didn't even want it anymore. The craving just started to fall away.

All this has really changed after my awakening. Now, there's no more judge or controller. So I've never been so free with what I'm putting in my mouth. There's no more judgment and there's no wanting to be different than what I am. There's just complete acceptance of the "what is," and no fear of becoming addicted. None of that is there. There's just complete freedom.

Filling the Existential Hole Inside

Biana Mavasheva, Awakened, Advanced Oneness Trainer, shares another aspect of what Deeksha offers those wanting to heal cravings or addictions:

Addiction is all about feeling an inner void, an inner emptiness. That inner emptiness, in Oneness and in many other spiritual traditions, has been called existential suffering, which is suffering that comes from feeling separate from life and from spirit. The Oneness Blessing returns us to an incredible fullness of spirit.

There's a sense of fullness when the love of the Divine rushes in. From that place, there is an inner wholeness because the void has truly been filled. Therefore, craving for a drug falls away naturally. There's no longer a need for some kind of substance to fill the inner loneliness. You now have the true solution, which is this extraordinary energy of love, peace, unexplainable joy, or even ecstasy running through your body, which the Oneness Blessing offers.

I personally had an incredible, mystical experience some years ago. An infinite, unconditional love awakened in me and healed any craving I had. The cravings were there to show me an inner emptiness and alienation from life because I didn't have that higher connection. Once the connection came, the cravings just naturally dropped away. The Oneness Blessing has allowed me to go deeper and deeper into this experience of love and ancient stillness, the essence of all life.

Space to Be the Inner Witness

Biana also mentions another important gift of Deeksha associated with a rise in consciousness and development of the inner "witness," which is that higher aspect of our being that observes the conditioned, clutching mind in operation without self-judgment:

> I've also seen cravings fall away in people because they begin to see the nature of that craving. The Oneness Blessing supports us in not being so entangled with the craving. There is space around it. There's awareness and we can watch it. From that watching perspective, we're able to relax deeper into it, and see what's there to teach us.

When we have the freedom to look at a craving from the perspective of that Higher Intelligence that witnesses, a helpful thing to do is to ask yourself a simple question: "What is it that I'm really wanting right now?" That's a way to begin to get in touch with the deeper feelings or needs underneath the cravings. Then you have an option to "stay with" those feelings and see the needs.

Biana has observed huge transformations in people who attend her Deeksha circles and courses:

> I've been in Oneness for about five years; I'm turning 30 now. I've witnessed in people a dropping-away not only of addiction, but also depression. I have to pinch myself because the transformation can be pretty radical. I've seen many people come to Oneness gatherings with so many struggles, despair, and a feeling that life is against them. They may go on to take the two-day Oneness Awakening course, and feel so transformed and healed from the work.
>
> Some people who've taken the course may temporarily return to that place of inner conflict and despair, but, inevitably, they see that it was an opportunity to heal any residue from trauma that they've accumulated. Oneness gives them the tools to process that trauma so they are no longer blaming others for their suffering, but owning it as something that lives within them. They have the tools now to sit with it and go through a process of healing.
>
> Sometimes I may not see these people for a couple of months after the course, but then when I meet them again, it seems as though I'm looking at a different person. I'm looking at someone who has a lot of light, hope, enthusiasm, and excitement

because they have returned back home. They feel that connection to spirit internally. They feel safe because they know their life is being guided by a Higher Intelligence. This isn't just an idea for them; there is a living of this experience. They trust life and relate to life from the connection within.

Biana's training and work is in the field of psychology. As she's mentioned, she sees the incredible potential of the Oneness phenomenon to help people transform psychological issues rapidly. She notes,

One of the missions of Oneness is to return people to their true essence, which is spirit. Many modalities do this, but Oneness does this effectively and quickly. The amazing gift of the Oneness Blessing is supporting us to heal and return back into a relationship with life that is fulfilling.

Because I've seen Deeksha be so effective for people who are struggling with specific cravings, one of my personal missions is to bring the Oneness Awakening Course to treatment centers. I'd like to conduct research on the effectiveness of this course in comparison to other therapeutic modalities.

The Science Behind Addiction and Deeksha

Another Awakened Oneness Trainer I talked with is an addiction specialist by training. Peter DeBenedittis, PhD, CPS, professionally does alcohol prevention work with high school students. Peter offers some insights from his own personal experience with addiction as well as a scientific approach to exploring the effect of Deeksha on the brain's role in creating addiction patterns:

When you look at the brain, and you look at how people who use drugs activate behavior, you see there are two competing systems in the brain: There's the Go System, which gives us rewards, like, "Eat when you're hungry," and then there's the Stop System, which says, "Danger, don't do that, there's going to be trouble."

For people who practice addiction, the Stop System never has a chance to activate. Their brains are wired in such a way that they'll see the stimuli that induces their craving and their brain will say, "This will be the best thing ever." They have this craving due to all the times they've used the drugs and built a lot of pleasure around that. The Go System activates even though, if they had a second to stop and think, they'd know that this may cost them their job or their wife, or something like that.

What I really like about Deeksha is that it slows the mind down. It creates a gap between an experience and the mind intruding on the experience, reactively telling you how you should act. That gap, from the standpoint of drug addicts, creates a little buffer that calms down the Go System when they have their cravings, so there's time to make a choice, rather than just react. They can respond by making a different choice, perhaps.

The gap that Deeksha creates allows the witness consciousness, the heightened awareness that Biana also mentioned, to come into play. In this gap is freedom from the mind's reactivity. Peter goes on to say,

What I've seen in my personal life is that the more I receive Oneness Blessings and move deeper in awakening, there's more gap; there's more time for me to have an experience without my mind coming in and automatically reacting.

I was a drug addict and a drunk for 20 years, so I know how this works. Even after I got sober and clean, I would still put myself in situations where my tendency would be to use. If I was emotionally uncomfortable, those were times I especially wanted to use. What I'm finding in Oneness and after awakening now is there's just not as much "oomph" behind the cravings. There's grace, and I've been relieved from that. I know from the neurobiology that what's going on is the gap is creating time for the Stop System to come in. I'm finding there's more and more relief from craving. This relief is the biggest blessing I've received as far as drugs, alcohol, and addictive behavior is concerned.

It's so common for all of us to feel shame and guilt after a bout of addictive behavior. It's such a part of the suffering we experience under the grip of a conflicted mind. We're often hard on ourselves due to the vast underpinnings of perfectionistic judgment endemic to our mental conditioning. Thus, the self-acceptance that comes naturally with increased awareness and awakening is an enormous gift of freedom and relief as well. The liberation from guilt and shame is another blessing Peter has personally experienced:

For the most part now, guilt and shame have pretty much been removed from my life. I might have a thought pattern that, in the past, I would have judged as terrible, as something I shouldn't do. Or I'll have a slight craving and feel ashamed. I used to have that all the time. Now, if I do have a craving, I just say to myself, "Okay, my mind is wanting this and I'm drawn toward it." I let my mind do whatever it's going to do. There's no shame and guilt afterwards.

That's a huge relief. I can say, "This is just my mind doing this again," or, "This is just a pattern I'm carrying," or, "Here I go expressing this again." But now I'm detached from the fact that I'm expressing it again, and don't believe that I'm a bad person because I'm expressing it.

Most of us have heard from experts how toxic and self-destructive shame can be, and we've also experienced its harm. Peter provides some interesting insights into how the downward spiral of shame and guilt reinforces itself and how awakening has disrupted that destructive loop for him:

In my experience, shame feeds the cycle of shame, and, very importantly, it also becomes its own reward. Having shame heightens the behavior when you do it. It builds up momentum to re-create the cycles so that when you do engage in the behavior, you get the guilty pleasure. There's actually pleasure connected to the shame in this way.

When you take shame out of the equation, you just observe yourself doing the behavior with some detachment. As I become more awakened, I can sometimes see the causes or I see that my mind is patterned to go down this road. When I'm not attached to it, I can actually choose whether to do it or not, and there won't be shame or guilt involved. That's been the biggest relief for me: to do what I normally do and not feel guilty about it! That takes all the pressure off it. Whether you call it an addiction, a pattern, or a pleasure, I was going to do it anyway, but now there's no more guilt.

Peter's experience in the spirituality-based program of Alcoholics Anonymous caused him to explore a possible scientific explanation for how cravings are said to be lifted for people who attend AA, as well as those who report relief through Deeksha. He says,

In Alcoholics Anonymous, a program that's saved my own life, they talk to you about grace; how your cravings will be lifted from you. I've seen this happen to many people, and wondered what changes a craving. I've looked at new research on how neural networks are built up, and how, over time, you pattern them and you become very good at these addictive behaviors. But if you consistently change your mental focus patterns, you begin to create different neural pathways.

I see that Deeksha is a way to shift into a new neural network. It leads to using a different portion of your brain, so the patterning of craving is not there because you make that shift.

I've actually seen real-time video of dendrites in the brain. The way they work is that they have little receptors on each end. At the molecular level, it's similar to a lock and key—this molecule fits into that one. Then, when the dendrite reproduces, the daughter cell will have the exact same receptors as the parent cell. That's why a craving stays and stays. But if there's a period of time of focused thought without a certain stimuli, the receptors that keep cravings in place will die off. So there is some biological evidence that you can shift your brain chemistry and be relieved of addiction. That shifted brain chemistry comes from mental focus.

Through my personal experience and my understanding of how Deeksha works, it's a shortcut, a fast shift to opening up the craving centers of your brain. It gives you awareness without your brain crowding in on that awareness. Deeksha seems to fit in entirely with all the studies on addiction and craving, and on all the brain chemistry documentation on addiction and craving.

We've known for a long time through AA that at a certain point, grace comes in. As we study it, we see that this grace is expressed through receptors in the brain dying off. We see movement in the prevention field, where they are using drugs to deaden those centers. But now we have a new technology available; we have a spiritual gift from the Divine to actually shift us into a place where craving is relieved. Being exposed to Deeksha is amazing because it creates a behavioral shift due *to the biological shift in the brain, without the use of drugs! We've come full-cycle back to grace, but now it's no longer struggling and hoping for grace. Grace is freely available and given in the form of a Oneness Blessing. That's why I'm excited about Oneness in my area of work.*

The potential for relief from emotional suffering, craving, and addiction seems absolutely limitless. Imagine a world where professional therapists, researchers, educators, addiction specialists, and healers of all kinds recommend Deeksha to their suffering clients! In the next chapter, we'll explore how the Oneness Blessing phenomenon can be helpful to healing the physical body.

CONTEMPLATION

Where does craving, addiction, guilt, and shame show up in your life? Can you visualize giving up self-judgment of these conditions?

CHAPTER 9

Health and Physical Healing

The root of all problems is getting emotionally stuck.
—Sri Bhagavan

Weekly Teachings, Week 195: June 8–14, 2014

After working as a massage therapist for 10 years, I suddenly developed back and nerve problems, which launched me in a passionate search for physical healing of these issues. The problem was so bad that I could no longer give massages. It was a big loss, for this was work I really enjoyed and that brought me a steady

153

income to supplement the shamanic healing I also did. I tried to find answers and a cure from numerous types of medical specialists and holistic practitioners, spending, from that time onward, thousands of dollars yearly on treatments. In addition to the considerable amount of money spent, I could no longer do many of my favorite physical activities or even sit on a chair for more than 30 minutes without going into spasm.

As a shamanic practitioner, I knew the importance of working on the spasm from a spiritual angle. From the shamanic viewpoint, physical symptoms start on the spiritual level and manifest emotionally and, ultimately, physically. Even knowing as I did that the physical expression of my pain and dysfunction had its origin in spiritual issues, I couldn't seem to access the cause, and my journey to healing became a long, persistent endeavor.

It wasn't until I found Oneness that the pattern of chronic spasm began to shift remarkably. In my first year of receiving Deeksha and attending Oneness courses, I noticed that the way I felt about the pain was completely shifting. I became very detached from it, and no longer felt so utterly depressed and victimized by it. I was enjoying life and just coping with the pain in various ways. But the pain was still there and I was still spending a lot of time and money dealing with it. It kept me from sitting comfortably and being as active as I love to be. Oneness had taught me to keep trying to pursue a healing of physical pain, and I did so because it was not a disability that I consciously wanted to accept. I was always praying for healing.

After 11 years of trying to heal this chronic problem, the first Sacred Chambers opened in my area: Kristin Panek's chambers in Downer's Grove, Illinois. I went there to ask my Divine for healing of my back. I felt that it would take a real miracle to end the physical pain I still experienced daily from back spasms. My prayer was, indeed, answered with a beautiful miracle.

A few days prior to visiting the Sacred Chambers, I had scheduled an appointment with a new chiropractor who had been referred to me. Within a few days after my visit to the Sacred Chambers, I saw him for the first session. He examined me, and I was shocked when he said that he thought there was a simple exercise that might control the spasm. He was correct. The exercise worked. Interestingly, this technique was one a physical therapist had tried with me 11 years prior, when the problem first appeared. It hadn't worked at that time, and no other practitioners or chiropractors had suggested it since.

A Matter of Energy

After speaking with Eric Isen, I had a better under-standing of why it took a miracle for my back to heal. Eric is an Awakened Advanced Oneness Trainer, Oneness Meditator, and Sacred Chambers Facilitator. He is a gradu-ate of Harvard University and has worked as an interna-tionally recognized Ayurvedic Medical Intuitive for more than 20 years. Eric is able to intuitively perceive the subtle energetic processes contributing to the health of his clients.

Eric confirmed for me what I already believed to be true from my many other experiences in energy healing. He said:

I use the Ayurveda system, which is the world's oldest system of medicine. The first line of the ancient Ayurveda scriptures says that every physical problem has a spiritual root.

Although Eric is not a physicist, his explanation of why this is so goes along with models of physics. This is an area where science and spirituality appear to intersect:

> The ultimate spiritual reality is nothing but oneness; it's a field of energy. That's all there is. This underlying field of energy forms waves. Those waves interact with each other and interference patterns, and they become more and more dense. That's how you get matter. It's all waves of energy. That is how this creation has emerged.
>
> Because your body is fundamentally made of energy, it goes through a series of energy transformations. It's the series of energy transformations that ultimately produce the physical body. The Prana, or energy body, is the immediate predecessor to the physical body.
>
> There's nothing but oneness, so what keeps you from living that, from being in a high state of awakening or even God Realization, or being pure light? Our charges keep us from that.

This concept of "charges" is such an important part of the teachings brought forward by Oneness University. The staying with the "what is," also called "holding" by Oneness University, is crucial not only to our happiness, but to the health of our physical body as well. Eric explains:

> Basically what happens is that our charges are like energetic knots that block the connection between the material and the ultimate energy, which we might call the Divine, or we could call Oneness.
>
> These energy blockages interfere with the proper formation and structuring of the body. People are born with different physical weaknesses because the energy flow that is structuring the body is disrupted by these charges. For example, if someone gets born with a weak liver, it's because some charge is interfering with the energy flow to that liver...or pancreas, or brain, or spine.

We may inherit these energy blockages genetically or they may occur due to karmic reasons (including past lives). In fact, Eric "looked" at my back issue, and told me its cause was karmic. We could all be born with a blockage that creates a tendency toward certain physical weaknesses from a past life or from our ancestors. Additionally, our experiences in the womb and early childhood conditioning, as well as unprocessed emotions during our lifetime, create charges (energetic blockages) that affect the health of our body. Oneness University and Oneness Trainers offer processes that help to dissolve karma and heal early childhood/womb experiences. By working to release the energy blockages from the womb and early childhood, we're also addressing karma.

Pure Attention Dissolves Charges

As Eric explains, the "holding" process (the staying with the "what is") is ultimately allowing our fundamental essence to dissolve the charges:

> Who are we? We are just oneness. The "holding" process allows you to take the mind out of play and let your attention—which is pure oneness, our highest nature—take over. When you can connect the charge with pure attention, it's going to burn the charge up. The oneness is like a fire. The charge is like pieces of old, dry wood. It's going to burn up. The attention is what burns it up. Your attention is oneness. It's only the mind that makes you think you're not oneness.
>
> In the ancient Vedic system, they call things like this "using a thorn to remove a thorn." You basically use the mind to destroy the mind. In ignorance, the mind is mostly functioning from charges. Even in the early stages of awakening, when the mind is declutched, it's still run by a lot of charges. It was for me. As you move along in your awakening, the

declutching becomes more and more pronounced. The mind becomes a very useful tool. It becomes like a friend, instead of a controlling enemy.

When you are successful in dissolving a charge by staying with the "what is," then there is an automatic wave of joy. This occurs because you have dissolved a blockage between you and the field of joy, which some may call the Divine. The sure sign of the presence of God is joy and bliss.

Whether or not one believes in God or some type of higher nature or force, there can be a very palpable shift in sensation when a blockage is released. This can be the wave of joy that Eric mentions, or it might feel like peace. The mind will become still. A transformation has taken place on an energetic level and it can translate to the physical body very quickly; a headache or stomachache may suddenly evaporate, for instance. Or there can be gradual relief of a symptom. As in the case of my chronic back spasm, there may be the appearance of what we call a miracle.

From a spiritual viewpoint, staying with the "what is" contributes to growing in consciousness. In a deepening of the awakening process, as the mind declutches and consciousness is changing, the physical body responds to this growth by coming into better balance. From a physiological viewpoint, a change in energy flow needs to occur in order for the body's organs and structure to function in a well-balanced fashion. As Eric says:

The charges totally relate to our health. If you're not dissolving these blockages, then you might be lucky enough to heal one symptom, but you're going to get something else. This is because the energy transformations that are creating the body are disrupted and imbalanced by our charges.

As we're able to progressively dissolve our charges and correct different functions on the energy level of the body, then the health problems will dissipate. It's easier to do this when you're younger. When you're older, it's harder to change the body. You might need to go to the Sacred Chambers; you might need a miracle.

In my case, as an older person with a karmic issue, I did need a miracle for the chronic back spasms. The charges contributing to my back issues are complex, and I am continuing to give and receive a lot of Deeksha, to stay with the "what is" to dissolve blockages, and to visit Sacred Chambers, praying for better and better health. As you will see throughout this book, the Sacred Chambers are producing a great deal of miracles all the time now, all over the planet. In Eric's words,

I think the Sacred Chambers are the most powerful, amazing gift we've been given yet. As that unfolds, as the miracles start to explode in numbers and in magnitude, we're really going to see a huge impact on humanity.

A Story of Miraculous Healing

Miracles of healing can start to happen just by getting your first Deeksha. David Tilove, an Awakened Certified Oneness Trainer from California, began a major healing process when he happened to see a notice about a Deeksha circle led by Eric Isen in 2006. Here's David's miracle story:

> It all began in September of that year when I was going through a divorce, got fired from my job, and had to move out of my home all at the same time. Needless to say I was a basket case. I also was on antidepressant medication, anxiety medication, and sleep medication. I had started on those medications 15 years earlier.
>
> At my yoga studio, there was a sign posted that said Deeksha would be given by Eric Isen and it stated what Deeksha could do for you. I had absolutely nothing to lose. So I went to my first night depressed and left happy. I didn't understand what it did for me, but all I knew is that I had to come back for more. The next week, I got more Deeksha; I cried at such a deep level and emotions began to come up and out. I said to myself that I had to get more

of this Deeksha; obviously it was doing something I had never experienced before, even in therapy.

So I found three Deeksha events to go to weekly from L.A. to San Diego. My life changed, and within three months I was off antidepressant medication, anxiety medication, and sleep medication.

In 2008 I went to Fiji to become a blessing giver so I could give back. In 2011, I went to my first deepening course at Oneness University, and more came up and out of me in 28 days than in 25 years of therapy. Then in September of 2012, I became a Oneness Trainer. I attended another deepening and became awakened on October 18, 2012, which is my actual birthday. What a gift of grace from my Divine! It has been a great ride for not only my healing, but also the healing of others in my life.

What to Do When You Get Sick

David's amazing story underscores the importance of discovering and staying with our repressed emotional pain in order to release the energy blockages and heal. Catherine Scherwenka, Awakened Advanced Oneness Trainer and Oneness Meditator, offers a great piece of practical advice to us all:

When there is emotional trauma inside, if you don't fully experience it and release it, it will come out in the physical body. The physical body is an amazing, magical computer. It can only tell the truth. So as soon as you get sick, you should automatically ask yourself, "What have I not fully experienced? What am I suppressing? What am I resisting?"

If you hold a request for clarity, joy, and healing, and ask your Divine, or ask what is sacred to you for help, the help will come. Oneness offers so many resources for becoming healthier on all levels.

CONTEMPLATION

Think about any areas or organs of your body that are causing recurring patterns of discomfort, tightness, or pain. Consider closing your eyes, slowing down your breathing, and focusing your attention on one of the areas. If you feel called to do so, stay with the "what is" of any emotions or sensations that arise as you focus on that part of the body and breathe. If you feel sensations drawing your attention to another location, you can focus on that other body part. Notice if emotions or sensations give way to joy or peace, or if the discomfort lessens as you focus for a while.

CHAPTER 10

Miracles Abound!

The Awakened One sees life as a miracle.
The unawakened one looks for a miracle in life.

—Sri Bhagavan

Weekly Teachings, Week 110: October 21–27, 2012

I n Oneness Blessing circles, one of the words heard with consistent frequency is *miracle*. The other frequently heard word is *gratitude,* for these two experiences are inseparable. At the most sweeping level, the phenomenon of awakening is the biggest miracle going on now. At the individual level, extraordinarily meaningful miracles seem to be as ordinary as the sun rising each day. The influx of this grace has many of us on our knees with humility and tremendous gratitude.

I described in previous chapters my own miracles with an 11-year-old chronic back spasm, the beautiful change in my relationship with my mother, and the unexpected opportunity to write this book, but the truth is, my life is overflowing with miracles now. For me, awakening has brought a change in perception that reveals the loving hand of Higher Intelligence in every detail of daily life.

The miraculous orchestration of events, awareness, shifts, and relationships reveals that everything in life is miraculously perfect, just as it is. We develop faith that life is sacred and good, despite the appearance of paradoxical atrocities and suffering in the world. Perhaps life can be seen as "perfect imperfection." In high states of awakening, we might see that all of this is just an illusion. But on the earth plane, there is very real loss, pain, grief, hatred, and the full range of human emotions and experiences. Yet, in staying with all these emotions of the "what is," we are returned over and over again to love, joy, growth, and peace. Looking back, we come to understand that there is purpose and design in the miraculous way life unfolds.

The Flow of Life After Awakening

Oneness Trainer and Sacred Chambers Facilitator Kristin Panek speaks of the awareness of this perfect imperfection of life's flow after awakening:

I feel like I'm much more in the flow. With this high energy here all the time, I'm juggling many more things at one time than I ever have in my life. My mind just freaks out if I stop and think about it, but the flow of how things happen is amazing. When I look back, I can see the flow of the contacts that I make and how they help with what's coming up next—everything is so beautifully orchestrated in that I can keep all these balls in the air and still keep on moving. It's clearly not me doing it because I could never figure all that out!

The other side of that is when I'm disconnected, it's much more painful. When I step out of the flow, or if I'm feeling hurt and believe the story about it, it's much more painful. So there's an incentive to drop into the experience and really be with it. The resistance is so much more painful.

"Flowering of the Heart" After Awakening

In addition to the change in perception of life's unfolding, there's a richness and depth of connection to others that is both ordinary and miraculous. After having spent so much of life feeling separate and conflicted, many people report a deepening of their relationships and having much more acceptance of others after awakening. Oneness calls this gift a "flowering of the heart."

Certified Awakened Advanced Oneness Trainer, Oneness Meditator, and Sacred Chamber's Facilitator C.J. Bigelow shares about the affect of the miraculous, yet ordinary "flowering of the heart" which is occurring in her family now:

In my family life, it means that people are just happy. It doesn't mean that we've changed that much, it's only that we've become so much more able to experience with each other how what once was irritating is now funny. This is a byproduct of a flowered heart. What you wanted before to be different in someone, you now just see it for what it is and think it's just endearing or funny. Or now there's a gentle teasing going on and the other person knows, from your tone of voice, that you notice it and it's kind of quirky but it's okay with you. That's real life. It's not high-minded.... It's all exceptionally ordinary.

Kristen Panek also speaks of the miracles in relationships she has witnessed as a Oneness Trainer and Sacred Chambers Facilitator:

I've seen many people's relationships shift. I've had people here who hadn't talked to their parents in many years. After being here for a while for Oneness Blessings, or after attending a Oneness

Awakening Course, either their parents call them out of the blue or they pick up the phone and call their parents. Huge shifts in family relationships have been happening all over the place.

Oneness Trainer, Oneness Meditator, and Sacred Chambers Facilitator Rev. Dr. Michael Milner speaks of the many changes in his family:

As our hearts flower in transformation, we experience deeper and deeper levels of connection with others, and genuine compassion begins to flower.

I had a very difficult relationship with my father, which really impacted my life. He was a wonderful guy, very loving, very charismatic, brilliant, very accomplished, but also very severe, judgmental, and abusive to me in my childhood. So I had a lot of wounds from that relationship, which of course affected everything. We know that the relationship with the father affects the flow of prosperity and abundance, and affects our relationship with our Divine. Though I had been working on it for many years, Oneness took the healing of my relationship with my father to a whole new level. As it happened, so much has taken place in all my relationships.

Suzanne, my wife, and I have been very careful not to try to indoctrinate or convert any of our family members to Oneness—although we live in a Oneness center, so it's everywhere—but we don't want to push it on anyone. Our children are just amazing. They are all in such wonderful states. Our youngest one is 13, the next is 18, and the others are both in their early 30s. We have such an amazing friendship that we share everything with each other. They are quite open to telling us everything going on inside. I never would have dreamed that possible a few years ago.

A Medical Miracle

As she mentioned, C.J. Bigelow is enjoying the everyday miracle of closeness and acceptance in her family relationships, but a desperate need for an extraordinary medical miracle occurred in her family several years ago regarding her son's health:

My son Eli had Legg-Calve-Perthes Syndrome. It happens to perhaps 1 in 2,300 kids, and 98 percent of those are boys of English descent. It usually happens between the ages of 2 and 10 years old. [In that syndrome], the ball of the femur in the pelvis breaks off and the bone dies and starts breaking off in a jagged fashion. It's a continual breaking-off process until it stops, and no one knows why it stops. But the moment it stops, the ball grows back. It's insanely painful. Every time it crumbles, it's like you broke your hip. My son had it in both legs. There were months when he couldn't walk. I was just sick about it. I was beside myself.

C.J.'s son was in agony and she was prepared to stop at nothing in order to help him. She called on her God, and God answered her. She was guided as follows:

Every night I said 108 Moola Mantras (a sacred Sanskrit prayer) to a glass of water, and every night my son drank the water. As a family, we were guided to sit on the bed with Eli in the morning. Eli would close his eyes. I would close my eyes and narrate an activity that Eli liked, such as soccer. I would narrate a game like I was a commentator. I'd say how Eli was playing, how he was handling the ball, how he kicked and passed the ball. I'd say that he'd go for the goal and score! Then my husband would narrate Eli jumping on the trampoline. In this way, Eli constantly visualized himself doing what he loved doing. He never thought of himself in any other way than perfectly healthy.

I also flew to India and participated in a group darshan with Sri Bhagavan. Sri Bhagavan blessed Eli and said, "He will play and walk normally."

Three weeks after that, my son was back in school, in the big yard, and he was kicking a soccer ball. I videotaped it!

We'd done X-rays when Eli was first diagnosed at age 5. He had complete deterioration by the age of 6 1/2. Usually that deterioration takes three to five years. And then he healed completely by age 8, with 100-percent bone growth and a return to full, normal activity. So from ages 5 to 8, he went through a syndrome that usually lasts anywhere from seven to 10 years. That is a total miracle!

There are many other stories of miraculous physical healings in Oneness, especially in connection to the Sacred Chambers. Awakened Advanced Trainer and Sacred Chambers Facilitator Cynthia Lamborne reports,

Just today I heard from a woman with a lot of physical pain, who had only had Deeksha once before, and came to the Chambers yesterday. She told me the pain was almost gone when she woke up this morning. For myself, I had eight weeks of a really bad bronchial pneumonia type of thing. I had a deep hacking cough whenever I laid down. But as soon as I went in the Chambers, it disappeared— it was gone when I came out of the Chambers.

A Prosperity Miracle

Many miracles of abundance and prosperity have been reported as well. Trainer Catherine Scherwenka talks about an amazing miracle that took place after she taught a Oneness course called the Wealth Process:

In October 2012, I taught the Wealth Process with Certified Oneness Trainer Mary Carroll from Wisconsin. During the process, one of Mary's prayers was that she somehow gets to the 28-day Deepening Course at Oneness University. She was leaving it purely up to her Divine because she has two children, a husband, a full-time job, she owns rental property, and her life is just very full. To get away for four weeks would be next to impossible.

So Mary said this prayer to go to Oneness University during the Wealth Process. For the 11 days following the course, you do an at-home practice that's very powerful. People get really hooked on the practice because it creates a lot of momentum and energy of abundance in all aspects of your life—not just monetarily. It really gets the energy moving in people's lives.

Mary was a few days into this at-home practice when she got a phone call from her father. He just said to her, "Hey, I want to let you know your step-mother is sending a check in the mail to you."

He didn't say for how much, and Mary figured it might be for a small amount like $25, and then she kind of forgot about it.

The week of Thanksgiving, the check came in the mail, and it was for $10,000! That check covered the cost of being in India for 28 days and the cost of being away from work for 28 days. That check allowed Mary to go and become awakened. There are many miracles like that from the Wealth Process that the Oneness Trainers teach.

A Miracle of Falling in Love

Valerian Mayega, Awakened Advanced Oneness Trainer and Sacred Chambers facilitator, met his life partner, Beth Murrell, an Awakened Oneness Trainer, at a Oneness Awakening Course four years prior to realizing his deep feelings for her. The couple credits the Divine for bringing the huge miracle of love to them. In fact, there was a cascade of miraculous events that brought them together. It all began when Valerian went on a journey from desperation and ignorance to awakening and cognizance. He credits Oneness for this:

My job and my marriage were ending. I was in the middle of a divorce, and disconnected from my children. I was in a really dark place in my life with many self-destructive habits and ways of being. I was like a tornado and collateral damage was all around me, but I was basically unaware and asleep. My brother had been inviting me to try Oneness, but I was resisting.

I had an opportunity to interview for a job, which involved working in Phoenix, Arizona, but because my kids lived in Dallas, Texas, I thought a good father should be near his kids, even if he was unemployed. Eventually, I had to surrender that concept and went to the job interview. Because I was afraid of flying, I had to take buses and trains to get to the interview. I was full of fear, anxiety, insecurity, total chaos, and confusion.

I got the job and relocated to Phoenix, and it turned out to be a gift from God. The Divine was working in my life, even if I wasn't aware of it. The company moved me there and even agreed to hire me as a Texas employee (because they had a site in Austin), so I wouldn't have to break the details of the divorce agreement. I began to read a lot, anything with a spiritual bent. All kinds of bad habits of eating and drinking fell away. After six months in Phoenix, the company unexpectedly said I could work from home in Dallas! What a miracle that I could be close to my kids again!

Back home in Dallas, I got into yoga and ended up taking a Oneness course. I was finally at the point of receiving—before, I was just resisting *everything. My mind had to be calmed so I could receive Oneness in my life. Looking back, I see the Divine was preparing me. I began to go weekly to Deeksha circles and gave blessings. Then I had the opportunity to go to India, but due to my fear of flying, I hadn't flown in 10 years. It came to me to pray, on the spot, to get over this fear of flying. So I did, and within five minutes, I could feel the fear lifting!*

At that time, the dream job had just ended, which opened the opportunity to go to Oneness University for a month. I became a trainer. I came home, taught a Oneness Awakening course, and met Beth in the course.

Later that year, nine people from their community, including Beth and Valerian, all ended up going to a Deepening Course at Oneness University and became awakened.

During that Deepening Course, Beth wanted to have the Oneness Guides do a Homa for her to meet a life partner (at that point, she and Valerian were still only friends). A Homa is an Indian ritual prayer for certain things such as health, finances, partnership, karma removal, and so forth. Beth had some money with her to pay for a Homa.

Valerian wanted to attend the Advanced Trainer Course, which was being held immediately following the four-week Deepening, but he didn't have enough money to pay for it. Because Beth was so grateful for the dedication and inspiration that Valerian had been providing the community as a Oneness trainer, she contributed her Homa money for Valerian's Advanced Trainer certification course. As Beth says, the Divine created a miracle for her:

> In contributing to Valerian and who he is as a person, and for the community, my Divine actually "gave me" him as a partner! It took about a year after that, but our paths kept intertwining.
>
> On some level, I was resisting partnership because I was on a yogi path. I didn't see Valerian as potential partner, although we shared yoga and Oneness. Everyone else in our community saw us together!

Beth and Valerian ended up going to a Sacred Chambers in the Aspen area of Colorado about a year later (still just friends). Valerian had been carrying a prayer for about a year for a life partner as well, and had been declaring to God, to himself, and to his friends that he was ready for a relationship. Their prayers were mirrors for each other. Their relationship finally changed after that Chambers event. Valerian says,

> My prayer for a partner was being worked on all along. Our paths kept intersecting, though we were focused on our own growth, and couldn't see anything else. We couldn't have done it without the

Divine, and it's the Chambers that took us both that last mile.

After walking out the Chambers, the entire weekend became a choreography and the Divine planned everything for us.

Beth says,

I had been looking for someone for three years, full of effort, and with nothing happening. When Valerian and I went to the Aspen Area Sacred Chambers, it was all natural and full of ease. It unfolded so naturally that I knew it was orchestrated somewhere beyond my own orchestrations, and landed in such a way that there was no fear, just recognition that this was a gift from the Divine.

Julia Desmond's Aspen Area Sacred Chambers has a specialty of wealth, abundance consciousness, and finances. We felt our miracle was abundant love and abundant time because we experienced abundant love that we felt for each other and for everything. It felt like time slowed down and we got to be fully present with each other, to really experience the other. That opened up the relationship even more. Maybe we had been so busy in our lives that we didn't have the time to really stop and be present with each other.

CONTEMPLATION

Ask your Divine (or whatever you think of as sacred) to reveal to you where you aren't receiving a miracle it's trying to give you. If desired, ask for help in receiving a miracle or more information on what you might need to do to receive the miracle you want.

event that characterizes permanent awakening. Later in the chapter you'll hear more stories about what it's like to live an awakened life, and get a glimpse into how some have experienced the mysterious moment of their neurobiological shift into awakening.

Awakening is basically the ability to stay with the "what is." Permanent awakening requires a neurobiological shift in the brain. The moment of the brain shift is only the beginning of transformation, for awakening has a momentum to it. After the shift in the brain, as awakening evolves with time, the levels of awakening increase, allowing longer and longer stretches of staying with the "what is" without effort. Because our minds are so conditioned to resist the "what is," in the lower levels or initial stages of awakening, there is often still some resistance that may require a bit of effort to stay with the "what is." but the effort largely takes the form of holding an intention to stay with the "what is." As awakening evolves, we are staying with the "what is" *naturally* for increasingly longer periods of time.

Prior to awakening, staying with the "what is" is extremely difficult, even with a strong effort to do it. More than anything, our minds want to avoid what is painful or unpleasant. It's the resistance to the "what is" that causes us such tremendous suffering. Once awakened, however, that universal Higher Intelligence is doing the heavy lifting; the mind is declutched and we are increasingly becoming more bonded with this Universal Intelligence (the Divine Within). Staying with the "what is" becomes an effortless happening in the higher levels of awakening. At that point, we are purely living in the flow of the sacred orchestration of our life.

Prior to permanent awakening, a person may have many episodes of awakened states, which are heightened states of consciousness, and not to be mistaken for permanent awakening. These heightened states are temporary, and are said to be connected to the rise and fall of Kundalini in the body. *Kundalini* is a Sanskrit term for the snake-like energy that, according to ancient Hindu scriptures, lies coiled at the base of the spine.

Kundalini is understood to rise upward through the *chakras,* which is another Sanskrit term, meaning "wheels of energy," or "energy centers." Kundalini is traditionally encouraged to rise through yoga, meditation, and chanting practices. When it rises and fully opens the crown chakra at the top of the head, one is thought to reach a state of enlightenment. Oneness courses and Deeksha circles usually include processes and meditations (such as the ancient Chakra Dhyana Meditation) to awaken Kundalini and open the chakras. Oneness teaches that once the brain shifts, awakening is permanently present and Kundalini cycles in a regular flow through the chakras. However, awakening is only the initial stage of transformation that eventually could evolve into full enlightenment.

Oneness University differentiates levels of permanent awakening from levels of consciousness. Awakening is specifically relevant to the duration of staying with the "what is" without effort. The term *levels of consciousness* refers to an expansion of the self. As the self expands, there is more of a complete experience of oneness. As expansion occurs, the self moves from only self-concern to concern for those close to us, to concern for one's society, then one's country, then the world at large, and then to the plants and animals.

A highly conscious, awakened person experiences oneness on all these levels. Consciousness may continue to evolve into God Realization.

Living an Awakened Life

Oneness teaches that when the mind is de-clutched, we see that what we once took to be our true self is actually a number of different personalities that comprise the ego. When we no longer identify with the ego, we *witness* the various personalities that express through our being. We may have a bossy personality or a stubborn personality or a timid personality expressing at different times. But these personalities are not who we are. Our authentic self is that sacred, unchanging essence that is one with the eternal One.

Because we identify increasingly less with the ego, awakening creates a sense of surprising emptiness inside, but emptiness of the *best* variety, characterized by inner stillness and peace at the core of our being much of the time. The mind isn't chattering away as it used to, when we were so often filled with inner conflict and anxiety.

Contribution from an awakened person flows from the heart, rather than from the ego. The mind becomes a servant of the heart, providing tremendous focus when needed. Awakened people display a natural humility because the heart, rather than the ego, generally fuels motivations and actions. At times, the ego will still rear its head; the difference after awakening is that we're self-aware of the ego in action. Once awakened, we feel a growing desire to give to others, which manifests for each in our own individual way. Simply by the fact of increased joy, loving relationships, humility, and living with a sense of purpose, awakened people contribute powerful goodness to the world. They seem to radiate energy and naturally influence the growth of consciousness in others. Oneness University teaches that one person who is in a high level of awakening will positively affect 100,000 other people.

The impact of permanent awakening is universal, whether you have a concept of a Divine or whether you don't have one. Rev. Mahaal Ajallahb, Awakened Oneness Trainer, Oneness Meditator, and Sacred Chambers Facilitator, has a wonderful description of what to expect in your life after permanent awakening:

It would be an expansion in universal consciousness, in awareness, in how you relate to life and life relates to you. You would start to have the kind of practical experiences of life and living from an internal stillness, an opening, where you're not conflicted inside.

The pains and aches you've been carrying, thinking they're just a part of life, start to fall away naturally and your outlook starts to take on a new life. You start to see life differently. You start to make sounder decisions and you're not looking to make judgments. What was before a mystical experience of having a gut feeling, this feeling now becomes an everyday experience. So you start to have a vision that is playing out with you and the people around you...that is more harmonious. You're finding resonance. You feel more satisfied and committed with everything and everyone.

Your internal experience is now flowing out in your external world. What you're experiencing inside starts to reflect back to you. You don't try to explain it, but it is something inside; you're really experiencing what it means to be peaceful inside. It's to have an experience of life outside the conflicted self, outside of trying to find something or someone to fill the gap inside. You feel fulfilled on the inside. Life is giving back to you as you share it with others. Magically, the people around you start to reflect it too.

We all see that we are having an experience of the One. No matter what it's called, we all experience the One being all things and no thing...we all come back to the experience of what is.

Sheri Greenstreet, an Awakened Advanced Oneness Trainer, describes herself as having once felt "stuck, unloved, alone, and the anger and resentment that I had carried for decades ruled my life." In 2012, two years ago at the time of this writing, she became awakened. This is what she says about her life now:

It has been a truly magnificent two years in this new awake state...I feel more awareness, clarity, and inner peace. Now there is trust in what I see and know intuitively. I have lost my anger, rebellion, and the blaming that has kept me from having a close and loving relationship with my parents. I had horrible hatred in my heart. I had felt abused and unloved. All of that has melted away into nothingness over the last two years; it has been a process of letting it go. It was not instantaneous, but it has been a complete healing of the childhood wounds.

The same process has happened with my feelings about my ex-husbands. There is forgiveness in all my relationships, where once there was complete resistance to forgiving. I had no clue three years ago how to forgive.

I am feeling loved now. I am fine with being unpartnered, and alone with myself. There is no feeling of lack or aloneness in me. I love myself now and this enables me to love people I never thought I could love.

I have a greater sense of purpose now—there is a plan and it is working always for my highest purposeful good. I am confident and satisfied with just being! I am able now to give up planning my life—what I will do and where I will be and for how long. We will never quit evolving. There is no having arrived at something, as we are always arriving somewhere.

Surrender

One of the states we continuously arrive at during the awakening process, as well as after awakening, is surrender. The word *surrender,* in the context of awakening, means to let go of resistance. We reach a surrender point through grace, just prior to the actual neurobiological shift, when it becomes clear to us that no amount of struggle on our part to reject the unpleasant aspects of reality is going to work. We come to see how much suffering our resistance is causing us.

We see that our mind is constantly trying to avoid anything painful and uncomfortable—especially the emotion of fear. We observe how helpless we are to change other people, our emotional triggers, and the happenings of our life. We marvel at the sneaky ways our ego distorts reality, by projecting our suffering onto others in order to control the vulnerability and hurts we feel inside. Oneness teaches us that we do not have to judge or change any of this (we *can't* change the way the mind works)—we just become aware of it.

Then, through grace, something absolutely marvelous moves in and like a huge sigh after tremendous effort and struggling, we let go. Suddenly, the universe is giving us the biggest gift of our life: We have an awareness that everything is perfect just as it is, and, in fact, blissful when fully experienced.

How is it possible for something that causes us pain to be blissful? Awakened Advanced Oneness Trainer, Oneness Meditator, and Sacred Chambers Facilitator, Rev. Dr. Michael Milner explains:

> The pleasant experiences and the unpleasant experiences are all part of life.... Life has always been extraordinary, but we just didn't see it. The reality of the present moment is bliss; it's heaven. If we're asleep, we don't see it. It's all absolutely perfect, just the way it is. When you awaken, you see that.
>
> Oneness teaches that everything fully experienced is bliss. Being in awareness, just simply living without analysis and without resistance, is Sat Chit Ananda—it's bliss. When uncomplicated by wanting it to be something else, the awareness of simply being is bliss.
>
> Reality is very paradoxical. It's the mind that's got us thinking it's all got to fit, but it doesn't. Sri Amma said that where all contradictions coexist, there is God.

How we get to surrender, and when it happens, is going to be different for each of us. Grace is behind it, lining up people and situations that bring surrender to our doorstep. Before awakening, surrender requires great effort. However, if we're holding the intention to awaken, consciously or karmically, then grace moves in when we're ready.

Ancient Hindu Scriptures, as well as other prophecies, have long predicted a huge rebirth for humanity. Hinduism speaks of four great cycles of ages through which the consciousness of humanity moves. The previous age and last of the four cycles, the Kali Yuga, was the age of greatest inner and outer darkness, marked by a consciousness of separation from the One. The Kali Yuga was said to have come to an end right around the same time that the Mayan Calendar was also ending. As you may remember, the Mayan Calendar came to an abrupt end on December 21, 2012, and people everywhere wondered if that meant the end of civilization.

Oneness University teaches that we are in a new age now, the Golden Age, which is a time of rebirth of civilization, of reawakening to our connection to the one sacred essence. It is a longed-for ending of the suffering caused by the overpowering control of the mind and the illusion of separation. It is a remembering of the power of the heart, the time for love and peace to flower in our lives.

Sri Amma and Sri Bhagavan had predicted that the number of permanently awakened people would reach a tipping point by the end of 2012, which would spark global awakening in massive numbers. That crucial number, 70,000 awakened people, was reached that year, and awakening began spreading like wildfire throughout the world. The numbers of awakened people have kept increasing since 2012. According to Oneness University, at the time of this writing in 2014, there are more than 2.3 million permanently awakened people in the world, and more than 1 billion in awakened states.

The rebirth of civilization has begun, and we are incredibly blessed to be living in the beginning of the Golden Age. As Sheri Greenstreet notes,

> We are all in this new awakening time, and each of us will come to this place of remembering and loving, each in our own time with love and grace, and without judgment. There is a Divine patience in charge and we are allowed to suffer as much or for as long as we get something out of it.

Before awakening, we are so identified with our suffering that we don't even see that it may be unconsciously serving our mind's need for avoidance, significance, or love. We don't see how unnecessary it is. Yet, suffering has been caused by the over-identification with the mind, and after awakening, when the mind is de-clutched, we have both clarity and capacity to let go of the suffering arising from resistance. We find that our needs are met naturally, and seemingly magically at times, in this new state of surrender.

Appreciation flows abundantly after awakening. We see the pointlessness of resisting the "what is" and experience the flow of grace that surrender brings. Surrender becomes a happening that arises from awareness. We are carried on the wings of grace into higher and higher levels of awareness, and the awareness delivers us into deeper surrender and freedom.

Oneness teaches that to *see* is to be free. We don't have to be anything other than what we are. Our freedom begins by no longer identifying with the mind. This doesn't mean we don't have pain and feel the whole range of human emotions; we do, and we'll certainly continue to encounter life's usual challenges—but our relationship to it all changes. Without the suffering caused by resistance, we can fully experience pain and move through it, returning to joy and peace.

Susan Leigh Babcock, an Awakened Advanced Oneness Trainer, told me how challenging it was for her to understand what was behind all the extremely painful events of her life. Though her childhood was not traumatic, in adulthood she inexplicably lost two life partners to early deaths, oversaw the care of both parents, each with debilitating illnesses, until their deaths, and then lost her business partner to an early death as well. In addition, she lost a few beloved pets, four young adult cousins, and a beloved aunt. Taking all of these deaths together, it's a lot of emotional pain to make sense of and integrate. Susan kept asking herself why all this was happening. She continually struggled with it, wondering if she were somehow to blame for attracting this or whether she was avoiding living her own life through the years of caregiving.

When she went to Oneness University, she heard one of the Oneness Guides give a teaching and tell a story that, with the help of abundant grace, completely ended all her struggle with the "why" of her painful adulthood. She was moved into deeper surrender and freedom. In Susan's words,

I heard this teaching: Surrender means to accept whatever God gives you—and to see that as the gift.

This was not a new idea. And by the way, I'd found plenty of grace and love and gifts in each of my caregiving assignments and even in the death events. There was beauty and profound depth in them. I had my first major awakening to other dimensions after the diagnosis of my husband. It was then that I began my serious quest for spiritual growth and knowledge. I deepened. But I also saw it as a marble cake. It was one cake, sure, but some of the swirls were light and some were dark. That was life. To see the whole cake as "the gift" hadn't yet happened for me.

And yet, through this teaching, it happened in an instant. Before the teaching, our guide had told us that when we suffer, our Personal Divine suffers, many-fold more than we do. "Really?" I thought. That really affected me. "So why, then, would our Divines allow us, or give us, these sufferings?"

Then he told this story: A young mother has to make a decision about having life-saving surgery for her infant daughter. This surgery will be traumatic and cause the baby many ripple effects throughout her life. The mother is acutely aware of this. Yet, she has no choice really because the only alternative is sure death. So, as a mother, she elects to have her baby cut open, her organs and bones pushed around, and subjected to anesthesia, recovery, painkillers, isolation from the mother's touch, and who knows what more. She makes a decision that results in immediate and terrible physical and psychic pain for her child. This decision, because of her keen awareness, would hurt her as much if not more than her child, at least psychologically.

Susan had an intense realization that finally triggered a release of the repetitive mental questioning of her pain:

That is what my Divine was doing when I experienced these losses in my adult life. There was my answer: in the definition of surrender and the story of the mother and the baby. My Divine was giving me these life experiences, and my Divine was feeling my pain at a magnitude of 100. I didn't need to know the answer anymore, because my Divine is a Divine Mother giving me life-surgery, and my job of surrendering is seeing the whole thing, not just parts of it, as "the gift." And just like that, it changed for me. It wasn't merely a psychological shift. It was a spiritual epiphany.

It is only because of the presence in my heart of my Divine that this teaching and this definition of surrender would transform me so completely. I no longer question my life, what happened to me,

or why I made the decisions I made. I no longer
question my God. I am grateful for having walked
through the valley of the shadow of death, because
of the sunshine on the path to the top of the moun-
tain that I now enjoy, and because of the light in my
life from my God. It's such a miracle that all the self-
doubt and second-guessing are gone now, replaced
by faith. I never knew what it was, faith, because I'd
never experienced it this way. I couldn't go get it. It
just happened. Thankfully—it just happened.

The Neurobiological Shift

The actual neurobiological shift into awakening will
be very different for each of us. For some, the shift will be
so subtle as to be barely noticeable, gradually integrating
over time. It's quite possible that many readers of this book
might already be awakened and are only suspecting it now
after reading the stories and descriptions we've included.
Perhaps we've given you words to describe changes you've
observed but didn't fully understand.

In the initial stages of awakening, you may be confused
by the numerous emotional charges that often arise, and
you may question if you're really awakened. As you stay
with the "what is" of the charges (see Chapter 1), they release, and that initial period integrates. It absolutely helps
to continue getting Deeksha and doing practices to support
transformation during periods of intense growth such as
the initial awakening. Of course, because awakening is an

ever-evolving process, there is no limit to the amount of involvement with the Oneness Phenomenon that any person may have; the choice is completely individual. If you are like me, however, and see that awakening is a delicious way to live, and because life only gets better the higher your level of awakening, you might find yourself eagerly saying, "Yes, please, I'll have some more!"

For others who are aware of being awakened, the actual shift may have been quite pronounced. Many people have reported becoming awakened after Oneness events, watching Oneness Meditations, and visiting Sacred Chambers. If you go to Oneness University, there are courses that certify awakening, or give you a date that you will awaken. For more information about this, please see the Resources section. The Oneness University Website, Oneness USA Website, and some of the trainer Websites supply links to course listings at Oneness University that support and certify awakening.

I had my awakening shift at Oneness University, where becoming "certified awakened" helpfully validated a distinct and unforgettable experience. The entire four-week deepening course led me to surrender and awakening, but my actual moment of the physiological shift came while I was asleep. In the early hours of one morning in the third week of the course, I woke from a deep slumber with a massive headache unlike any I'd ever experienced. I'd never had migraines or anything remotely similar. The headache kept persisting and was so painful that I prayed desperately for relief. Within seconds of prayer, my personal Divine clearly instructed me to walk out the door and ask someone for Deeksha.

I got myself out of bed and stumbled out the door. There, walking just a few feet away was Julia Desmond, an Awakened Trainer and Oneness Meditator. I asked Julia for healing Deeksha, which she gladly gave me. My headache disappeared immediately after Deeksha. I knew with certainty that something was very different besides the absence of pain: I was filled with a happy calmness, and some things that had been triggering me at the time just dissolved into peace. Life felt effortless in the days and few weeks that followed, and then I, too, hit the fairly common initial period of strong emotional charges, which subsided after a few months as transformation continued (and is still continuing) to unfold. I have to chuckle at the mysterious drama of my awakening. I think my Divine knew I needed a proverbial thump on the head to satisfying skepticism. I had to have something concrete to occur that would give me irrefutable physical evidence of the shift.

Everyone's awakening will be unique and exactly how they need it to be. Debra Apsara, Awakened Advanced Oneness Trainer and Sacred Chambers Facilitator, physically felt her shift as well. This is what happened to Debra:

When I became awakened at Oneness University, I actually felt the process. I had gone to the special deepening course and at one point, I got a clear inner message that I could have awakening if I wanted. Of course I said yes, I wanted awakening, because I was a seeker, even though I wasn't even sure what awakening was. In that moment, it was like I was hit with a brick. It actually knocked me to my knees. It felt like there was a burning circle on the left side of my head, above my eye. As it burned, it seemed like a knife went into it. Then it moved into my third eye area, and then it was done. Afterwards, I got up and got the inner message that I was awakened. The guides checked, and, sure enough, I was awakened.

By the next morning, when I opened my eyes, everything was clearer. I'd had enormous existential suffering through my childhood, and through adulthood, and when I opened my eyes that morning after awakening, the existential suffering was completely gone. I had a clarity that I'd never had in my life. There is very little existential suffering for me now because I am so close to my Divine and I don't feel that state of separation as before.

For Catherine Scherwenka, an Awakened Advanced Oneness Trainer and Oneness Meditator, her awakening occurred at Oneness University in what is called Sacred Space, a dark room where she could be alone in her process. Catherine brings up a point that is true for everyone: awakening delivers each of us right into the heart of ordinary life. As we settle in to awakening, we see that we are more firmly planted in the *ordinariness* of everyday life, while our responses to life's events are subtly, but profoundly different. As she describes,

I was in Sacred Space for my awakening at Oneness University for three days. I was really surprised at the fact that I had no fear. I thought I'd have a lot of fear. When awakening was happening, things were very mystical, and I'm not a mystic. I recall having visions, with lights coming out of my eyes, and seeing different shapes, and feeling a very huge presence in the room I was in.

But when I got out of the Sacred Space, I called up Oneness Guide Doug Bentley and said, "They made a mistake. I'm not awakened!" I said that because everything still felt very much the same. And that's what awakening is—your life is very much the same, but you start to notice subtle changes, especially in your responses to things. You no longer react so much. You take a breath, and in that breath, you're able to respond instead of react. It seems so subtle, but it's so profound when you reflect back on your life. You see how you have been acting or reacting to things your whole life. You see that after awakening, there's that breath, and you're able to respond with awareness, intention, clarity, and reality. Your response is not from a trigger that creates a reaction that comes from an old story you are carrying in your mind. Your response no longer comes from that place.

This is one of the many profound blessings that come from awakening. It grows deeper and deeper as the months and years go on. Your experience of reality as it is really comes true. There's no more commentator of the mind. There's no more old stories getting rehashed, diluting your experience. It's just experiencing each moment as it is. It's profound.

I've been visiting family for the last month. It's always good to hang out with family to see how enlightened or unenlightened you are. And it's been really cool to watch my response to things that, in the past, would have just shot me out of my body, and, instead, I've been able to really stay present and aware. It's amazing. Your mom is still your mom and your dad is still your dad, but you don't have that knee-jerk reaction like you used to have. You're able to just observe and be a witness, and then respond.

Rev. Dr. Patricia Keel, Awakened Advanced Oneness Trainer, Oneness Meditator, and Sacred Chambers Facilitator, shares about the deep silence that characterized her moment of awakening:

I absolutely knew the moment permanent awakening occurred. I felt like someone had taken a laser light and made a circle around the top of my head and lifted the top of my head off. Everything went totally silent, so silent for a really long time. I was in the dark and noticed there was some aspect of consciousness that was looking down inside this empty head, trying to find a thought, and saying, "Is there a thought in there? I can't see one in there!"

That was my experience of the permanent shift into awakening. From that moment on, the stillness and silence has been pervasive. When the mind is needed, it comes, but when it's not needed, it doesn't come.

Rev. Dr. Michael Milner also speaks of a laser penetrating his head during the moment of permanent awakening:

When it happened for me, I was in what's called Sacred Space, in a dark room at Oneness University, and I was fully aware. I asked Sri Bhagavan to let me be fully aware in that moment and experience what would happen. So I have a take on what was done in my brain, what changed and what didn't. It was very clear to me that I was in a state of deep helplessness. It hit me like a ton of bricks that there was nothing I could do.

When the Divine came in, Sri Bhagavan was there with me in spirit and he said, "Now we begin."

When I'd reached this point of complete broken-ness and helplessness, and surrender happened, it was like a laser that went right into my brain core. It was like surgery. Something very minute dissolved. Then Sri Bhagavan said, "So what's there now?" I said, "Helplessness." But I couldn't find the "I am helpless" at the center of that. Helplessness was still there. Everything was the same, but the one who was suffering with that, the one who was resisting, the one who was craving for it to be different, was gone. That was the psychological dimension to it, but something physically was dissolved, and it was deep in the brain core. I don't know what it was; all I know is I watched it being done and I felt it.

Being awakened is really just awareness of the "what is," without resistance to whatever is, which can be pretty crappy sometimes or it can be wonderful. But there's no resistance to it, whatever it is. In fact, there's no ability to resist it anymore. Some people, after they initially awaken, experience a Mt. Vesuvius of charges coming up and they're blown away. There was a part of them that had been able to resist and run from the charges. Whatever that was, that little thing is missing after permanent awakening.

Whatever it is in us that resists reality as it is, and craves for it to be something different, that part dissolves progressively at a deeper and deeper level as awakening unfolds. Nothing really changes in the world, but it's the way that we're experiencing the world that dramatically changes.

Rev. Dr. Michael goes on to provide some further insight into awakening using the wonderful metaphor of a door that separates the mind from the "what is":

Another way to look at it, which I really like, is that we're either in the mind or we're in the "what is." And the mind is the cause of all the suffering.

When some of us first experienced awakened states, for one reason or another, a door opened and we found ourselves passing out of the mind and into the "what is" for a period of time. That was bliss! A lot of us went, "Wow, I'm awakened, I've arrived," but only too quickly, we were cast out of the garden, and back into the mind, back into an ordinary state. The door slammed shut and locked. Then we were beating against that door, trying to get back into pure awareness outside of the mind. For a while, most of us believed it was our spiritual practices that made that door open, so we doubled up on our meditation, or whatever we were doing; we did even more of it. But it has nothing to do with our efforts; it's pure grace that opens the door.

What we eventually discover is that we can't do anything to open that door. It opens from the other side. We give up. When we truly give up—not out of laziness, but when we've done everything we can possibly do, and reached the end—then Divine intervention comes. When that happens, the door doesn't just open; the Divine tears the door right off its hinges and throws it away. So now you've still got these two rooms, the mind and the "what is," but there's an open doorway in an awakened person.

Rev. Dr. Michael goes on to explain why the initial stage of awakening can be confusing, as we witness ourselves still struggling with resistance to the "what is" at times:

In the beginning, for an awakened person, that is the only difference: there's no longer a door that you frustratingly cannot open. Now, after awakening, there's just an open doorway you can go through any time. But because of a lifetime of conditioning and habits, newly awakened people spend most of their time in the mind, struggling in the beginning.

Then one of us comes along and taps them on the shoulder, asking, "Why are you struggling with that? There's no door there anymore!"

So with the slightest effort, with just taking an intention, you can leave the mind and go right into the "what is." But because we don't know how to live that way, because we have all these habits and patterns, we keep going back into the mind. So in the beginning, we have to be reminded to keep making that little bit of effort. Then it starts to become effortless and we start spending more and more time in the "what is" and less time in the mind. That is the process that leads to full awakening.

Awakening is simply when a change takes place such that there is no longer a shut door to the "what is." Something has happened inside the brain that we don't understand yet...something at the very center of our experience of reality has dissolved, and it's so subtle that it's possible to not know it's happened.

It's a beautiful paradox that the very state of helplessness Rev. Dr. Michael talks about is what grace needs to pull that door to freedom off its hinges.

Awakening is a glorious and unmistakable mystery that is yours to have if you want a real adventure. In the following, final chapter, should you decide to take up the adventure, you will find some aspects of the Oneness Blessing Phenomenon, available in addition to Deeksha, where the "what is" shows up in all its mysterious glory.

CONTEMPLATION

How is resistance showing up in your life? What relationships and situations trigger strong emotional reactions? Can you see these as an invitation to deeper surrender?

individual to find his or her own unique, direct revelation of whatever path, religion, or experience is solely right for him or her.

Emerging in the 1980s from a small town in India, and continuing to have a huge and rapid global impact on people's lives, this gift is quietly but powerfully paradigm-shifting. It all began with the vision of Sri Amma and Sri Bhagavan, and a Deeksha given by their son Krishnaji to schoolmates. Now we have a phenomenon that catalyzes for humanity what it wants and needs most: liberation from suffering. I think about the lifetime I've spent searching for happiness and wholeness, and the centuries of searching and suffering endured by my ancestors, and I'm in awe that such a priceless gift was delivered to us now by grace, at a time when we really do need a miracle to save this planet.

For the cynics and skeptical thinkers among you, I have no more to offer in the way of proof of this gift's power than to say, "Try it." You really have absolutely nothing to lose. We've already collectively lost so much of value to the consequences of rampant greed, aggression, and inhumanity. Even if you appreciate miracles and grace, chances are that deep down, you might believe that we all have to create our own happiness and success by the sheer force of our will. You might also unconsciously believe that happiness and success are possible for others, but not you.

Can you make room in your heart for an infusion of grace and an everyday miracle for yourself? Would you like to become awakened? The only price to pay is the dawning awareness of how powerless we are to change the nature of our collective mind that has created all these ageless problems. I recommend that you just be curious. See if there's something there for you that you couldn't even imagine, something that is your birthright. Because I can assure you there is, though you have to experience it yourself to know it.

You may have to experience grace over and over until you can fully digest its nourishment; that's simply the nature of skepticism and the mind. The knee-jerk patterns of doubt are deeply ingrained. We don't typically welcome feeling helpless or surrendered. We've gotten pretty darn comfy with our illusions of control, which can so efficiently camouflage grace's often subtle footprint.

Deeksha and Oneness Meditation

I encourage you to receive Deeksha, if you haven't tried it. There are numerous Oneness Blessing circles that gather weekly throughout the world and in most major cities of the United States. You can also explore Oneness Meditations given by Oneness Trainers who have been initiated to share Deeksha through the eyes. It may sound a little strange, but when you experience this phenomenon, you'll likely feel the powerful energy that flows so abundantly.

In-person sessions of Oneness Meditation (also referred to as OM) are harder to find in many locations because there are only several hundred Oneness Meditators throughout the world. But many of these specially initiated people offer free, weekly online webcasts of OM. Day and night, seven days a week, you can watch one of these online broadcasts from countries all over the globe. Many of the Oneness Meditators who have contributed to this book broadcast weekly. Please see the Resources section for

Websites that offer links to scheduled Deeksha circles and Oneness Meditations.

I remember the very first Oneness Meditation event I attended. North America Oneness Coordinator and Oneness University Guide Doug Bentley was introducing OM in the United States for the first time, one summer weekend in 2012, in Washington, D.C. I hadn't yet been to Oneness University, and was not awakened, but the blessing of this experience gave me a blast of the awakening process that began unfolding in the months that followed.

At the event, Doug's eyes, his face, and in fact his entire being, radiated such incredible love, humility, and beauty that I was overwhelmed with gratitude and feelings of pure bliss. I didn't know what to make of the profound sense of divinity that took me by surprise, but I could feel the power of its revelation. During the experience, many of the audience members laughed or cried with joy and gratitude, as Doug transmitted sacred energy through his eyes, while flashing a range of emotions across a radiant face.

In talking with a number of Oneness Meditators since then, I've learned that their own personalities disappear while sharing OM. C.J. Bigelow, who is an Awakened Advanced Oneness Trainer, Oneness Meditator, and Sacred Chambers Facilitator, describes it like this:

> Being a Oneness Meditator, I'm being used by the Oneness Phenomenon in a really specific way... it's almost like the eyes of a Oneness Meditator are a mirror for you to see yourself. The Oneness Meditator is completely stepping aside and the

body vessel becomes this grace. And that grace is your mirror for you to experiment with, dance with, embrace, and become it, so you can have this deep experience of the Divine.

Rev. Dr. Michael Milner, also a Oneness Meditator, Awakened Advanced Trainer, and Sacred Chambers Facilitator, shares what a blessing it is for him to be a Oneness Meditator:

When I'm giving the Oneness Meditation, the Divine just consumes me. I don't breathe most of the time the Oneness Meditation is happening. I'm in a breathless state. The Kundalini comes right up to the crown chakra, the breath stops, and my eyes don't blink for however long it lasts. It's pretty amazing.

I'm a teacher and I was a minister for decades. To be able to sit in silence now with a group of people with their eyes wide open and say nothing, and have them experience the Divine in a profound way, is just a fulfillment of my heart's desire.

Catherine Scherwenka, also a Oneness Meditator and Awakened Advanced Trainer, speaks of the experience of being taken over when she gives OM:

When I'm sharing the Oneness Meditations, I'm completely taken over by the Divine energy, the Creative Intelligence, or whatever name you want to give it. There's no mind, no commentator, no judge, or controller there. I don't feel the body. My body is not my body. I feel like I'm in Samadhi, and the experience changes every time.

It must depend on many variables, like the crowd of people, or the energy of the area, as well as myself. Something internally in me may affect it because sometimes it's very deep, where I know I barely move or breath, and there's just a huge energy coming through. Other times, there's a lot of laughter or tears, but it's nothing personal. I always preface each OM by telling the audience that if you see me laughing, it has nothing to do with the person I'm looking at. It's just energy coming through.

The Sacred Chambers

If you've read this book chapter by chapter, you're familiar with the stories included from people who have experienced miracles either during their Sacred Chambers visits or afterwards. Catherine Scherwenka says about this newest development in the Oneness Blessing Phenomenon,

The most exciting thing of the moment is the launch of what is called the Sacred Chamber Process here in the West. The intention of this new process is to connect us more deeply with the Divine, Higher Self—whatever name you want to give it. This powerful energy is what resides inside the Chambers.

When people enter the Chambers, they have miracles, huge deepening with their Divine, healing of their relationships, insights, and enormous love and gratitude. There are active Chambers spread across the planet, and the phenomenon is growing rapidly, changing people's lives.

Debra Apsara, Awakened Advanced Trainer and Sacred Chambers Facilitator, passionately speaks of the gift of the Chambers:

It has been the greatest gift ever given in my whole life, and probably prior lifetimes on this planet. I feel incredible gratitude to be able to open the door so people can go into the Chamber rooms and sit with this kind of beautiful energy; to help them grow and heal, and all of those things that are in that healing chamber. To be part of a generation where the state of humanity's consciousness is changing is beyond my wildest dreams—I am at a loss for words for all the gratitude I feel.

Rev. Dr. Patricia Keel, Awakened Advanced Trainer, Oneness Meditator, and Sacred Chambers Facilitator in northern California, speaks of the preparation Chambers facilitators go through to hold this grace-filled process for others:

When people go into the Sacred Chambers, they are going into a dedicated space that has been prepared and prayed for. They have been prayed for that they are going to have a connection with something greater than they have ever connected with before, or to be able to deepen that connection.

I wish I had a camera, because sometimes people come out of the Chambers with their eyes really wide. There might be this look on their faces like, "I don't know where I've been, and I have no idea where I'm going, but I'm here right now and I can't move!" There's something that happens to people when they go into the Chambers and it's something they connect with...they've connected with something very deep, some old story or picture, or something they've been looking for their whole life. Or they're in such a state of bliss and joy and grace that they can't even speak.

Many of the Sacred Chambers have specialties that have been revealed to the facilitators. For instance, Kristin Panek, an Awakened Advanced Trainer and Sacred Chambers Facilitator, says this of her Chambers near Chicago, Illinois:

> I've known since the beginning that the Chambers I facilitate were about healing relationships. Part of the reason was the way it came to be—that it healed ours [her relationship with husband Frank]. I've seen many miracles in that area. People write me afterward about how their relationships with their partners, or their parents, or their kids have shifted as a result of coming, even if they had come to the Chambers for a different reason. It just became a part of what they were receiving.
>
> Working with people to heal relationships has been a major piece of my own work in the last many years, too, so it all fits...with the Chambers, there is nobody in between—it's just them and the Divine, and the Divine puts them through whatever experience is needed for their healing. Or they come out of the Chambers having been healed. The Divine has so many different ways of supporting people in their process, but there's no middle man. They just go in and the Divine runs the show. It's a leap to the next stage of healing.

Rev. Dr. Michael Milner has a Sacred Chambers in Clearwater, Florida, in the Oneness Center he hosts with his wife, Rev. Suzanne Champlin (also a Oneness Trainer). He speaks of the many physical healings in the Chambers of injuries and chronic illnesses. Additionally, he says,

> I'm seeing a lot of flowering of the heart happening...healing of the things that have been keeping people bound up in their relationships and their spiritual path, and things that have been keeping their hearts constricted.
>
> I love taking people through the Chambers. The kind of breakthroughs they're having now used to require going to India. The teachings at Oneness University are absolutely amazing and life-changing, but if you can't go to India, there are some parallels to what happens in the Chambers and what happens on the different floors of the Oneness Temple [at Oneness University]. Now people can have an experience that's like being at the Oneness Temple in India, but it's in the Chambers here. They can have the insights and clarity and closeness to their Divine.

Rev. Dr. Michael mentions that the three rooms that comprise every Sacred Chambers have parallels to a number of different spiritual traditions:

For example, there's a parallel to the three courts of Solomon's Temple: The outer court was a place of instruction. The inner court was where the priests would purify and cleanse themselves to go into the Sanctum Santorum, the Holy of Holies. That three-chambered process of approaching the direct manifestation of the Divine is something that you find in the Hebrew tradition, in Freemasonry, and in many of the ancient mystery schools. This is the way into the deep, mystical experience of the Divine. It mirrors all the mystical traditions of the world.

You can find a Sacred Chambers to visit by checking the Resources section. Reservations are needed to attend, and there is no cost. Some of the Chambers list their specialty, but one can bring any intentions and prayers to all of the Sacred Chambers throughout the world. Going to a Sacred Chambers is such a unique way to have a rapid, direct, and personal experience of that which is sacred to you, free of any intermediary's interpretation or limitations.

The Future

The gift of direct experience, of revelation without any intermediary, is significant in that it offers every individual an opportunity for pure *awareness* of the "what is." One of the biggest teachings of Oneness University is that awareness is not a means to obtain something else; it is an end in itself. To this point, although it is good to choose one path to guide you toward the awareness that *is* permanent awakening, any path that you choose to follow must eventually drop away as each individual is ultimately living in the "what is" without conditioned concepts and images. To live life fully like that is beyond the mind, beyond what we can understand through thinking, yet that is real freedom.

In the meantime, until our paths, religions, teachings, and even the practices of the Oneness Phenomenon drop away because we no longer need them, we're part of an extraordinary time of massive growth and transformation. Becoming aware is a huge adventure, always filled with many surprises.

The Oneness Blessing Phenomenon epitomizes this, for it continues to transform at such a rapid pace that I suspect by the time this book comes out in print, even newer developments will be revealed. In the past year, one development of the Oneness Blessing Phenomenon that was actually held as a vision by Oneness University for some years has started to become a reality: the birth of Golden Age Villages. The "Golden Age" refers to the age of awakening, the last of the four great cycles of humanity that we have just entered, as discussed in ancient Hindu scriptures (see Chapter 11: Awakening).

Oneness University teaches that first each individual becomes one within themselves. Then each person inspires and contributes to society becoming one, and ultimately the world becomes one in this way. So the next step in the evolution of oneness points toward a "village" with each member contributing to the good of the community, honoring the natural ecology of the location, and sharing a vision of oneness. It would be a place for awakening, transformation, and God-realization. It is expected that there will be 108 of these villages, located all over the world, to help bring the planet into a state of collective oneness.

Rev. Dr. Patricia Keel describes what a Golden Age Village will include:

> The villages will have certain elements in them. The central element of the village will be a meditation hall that will hold the Presence as the people in the community who build it know that Presence. That will be the center of this village.
>
> The village may have a school. It will have a place for people who want to raise beautiful, awakened children. It will have a place for birthing those children. It will have a place for people who want to make their physical transition from a very sacred place where people are celebrating their moving on into higher states. It will be like a hospice for higher consciousness. So there will be both ends—birth and death—as part of the village. There will also be a healing clinic in the village, which will be a big piece of it.
>
> There will be a place for people who want to go on spiritual retreats. There will be a place for teachers who want to lead Oneness teachings. Other spiritual leaders and teachers will also come. People will come to give lectures and workshops. There will

be yoga classes and dancing and ritual. There will be water on the property so people can do things on the water. There will be another area beyond retreat space that will be like a resort, where people can come and spend a month, or two weeks, and really enjoy the property and partake in classes or workshops if they choose to.

So there will be a retreat quality, a spiritual teaching quality, a resort/relaxing in nature quality— places to hike and just enjoy the property. There will also be people in very high states who will actually be living on the property. They may be living there in single-family houses or may be living in some kind of communal housing. They may be there with their families. It will be a place for people of all ages to come and enjoy.

It's already started in Hungary. A man heard about the vision of Golden Age Villages and bought 500 acres in Hungary with a hospital and a school. It will be like a spiritual oasis.

In North America, Awakened Oneness Trainer, Oneness Meditator, and Sacred Chambers Facilitator Julia Desmond is the Project Manager for the Golden Age Village in Colorado. A large parcel of land has been purchased in a beautiful and sacred location in the Rocky Mountains, and is in the first phase of development. This is the first established Golden Age Village in North America, and Oneness programs will be offered there in 2015. For more information, please see Julia's Website, listed in the Resources section.

Rev. Dr. Patricia and some others are holding a vision for a Golden Age Village in the San Franciso Bay area. They hold a weekly visioning call to envision villages all over North America. For more information, you can find Rev. Dr. Patricia's contact information in the Resources section. The visioning is already attracting people, she says:

> I'm getting people who want to help with the real estate, I'm getting developers contacting me, and an architect e-mailed me today. All I'm doing is holding the vision.

A vision is a very powerful thing. After awakening, it's clear that how we perceive the world is how the world will be for us. As we peer at the perceptions that arise from fear and stay with the awareness that arises from the "what is," our heart's vision emerges to take the lead. We move into the now moment, opening to the sacred orchestrations of grace.

As we've said throughout the book, awakening doesn't prevent the unfolding of life's usual challenges, but what changes very naturally is the way we live and flow with life. When the inevitable challenges arise, we handle them differently; we can relax into stillness and inner guidance that navigates us through the choppy waters. As emotions are experienced fully, without resistance, we are gently returned to joy and peace.

Please know that a huge number of people are holding a vision of full awakening for all of us, and liberation for all the beloved ones who have come before us. For those who will blessedly inherit a new consciousness of oneness in generations to come, may they only know of suffering by reading about it in history books!

CONTEMPLATION

Are you beginning to trust in a universal higher consciousness, or essence, that has invited Deeksha into your life, which has your back, and is completely in favor of your happiness? Ask now that this sacred essence give you a direct experience of its grace.

Resources

Oneness University Websites

- **OnenessUniversity.org:** general information on courses and programs
- **OnenessUSA.org:** courses, trainer listings, Sacred Chambers listings, and Oneness University applications for only United States and Canada
- **WorldOnenessCommunity.com:** general Oneness information, lists of international Websites by country, social networks

- **WorldOnenessFoundation.org:** to make a tax-deductible donation

Contact Information for Certified Oneness Trainers in This Book

- Rev. Mahaal Ajellahb, Awakened Trainer, Oneness Meditator, Sacred Chambers Facilitator: Waterville, Maine; angelsrus7@gmail.com, *www.evolveandlead.com*

- Debra Apsara, Awakened Advanced Oneness Trainer, Sacred Chambers Facilitator: debra.apsara@gmail.com

- Susan Leigh Babcock, Awakened Advanced Oneness Trainer: Woodstock, N.Y.; susan.babcock@gmail.com, *www.omdeplume.com*

- Cynthia (C.J.) Bigelow, Awakened Advanced Oneness Trainer, Oneness Meditator, Sacred Chambers Facilitator: Santa Monica, Calif.; cj.bigelow@mac.com, *www.socaloneness.org*

- Mary Carroll, Awakened Oneness Trainer, Milwaukee, Wisc.; marycarroll824@gmail.com, *www.onenessmilwaukee.com*

- Peter DeBenedittis, Ph.D., CPS, Awakened Oneness Trainer: Santa Fe, N.M.; pdebenedittis@medialiteracy.net, *www.medialiteracy.net*

- Julia Desmond, Awakened Oneness Trainer, Oneness Meditator, Sacred Chambers Facilitator: Colorado; *www.juliadesmond.com*

- Sherylynn (Sheri) Greenstreet, Awakened Advanced Oneness Trainer: Dallas, Texas; communityseulcoeur@gmail.com

- Eric Isen, MSCI, Awakened Advanced Oneness Trainer, Oneness Meditator, Sacred Chambers Facilitator: La Jolla, Calif.; emisen@mac.com, *www.ayurvedicintuitive.com*

- Rev. Dr. Patricia Keel, Awakened Advanced Oneness Trainer, Oneness Meditator, Sacred Chambers Facilitator: Kentfield, Calif.; patriciakeel@gmail.com, *www.patriciakeel. com*, *www.onenessprogram.com*, *www.unity.fm/ program/onenessprogram*

- Cynthia (Thia) Lamborne, Awakened Advanced Oneness Trainer, Sacred Chambers Facilitator: Encinitas, Calif.; Cynthia@onenesssandiego.com, *www.awakeningsandiego.com*, *www.atlasbalancingusa.com*

- Biana Mavasheva, Awakened Advanced Oneness Trainer: Skokie, Ill., biana@ onenesscenterchicago.org, *www.agorahub.com*, *www.meetup.com/onenesschicago.com*

- Elizabeth (Beth) Murrell, Awakened Oneness Trainer: Tempe, Ariz.; onenessbeth@gmail.com, *www.beamesyoga.com*

- Valerian Mayega, MSEE, Awakened Advanced Oneness Trainer, Sacred Chambers Facilitator: Tempe, Ariz.; valerian@gmail.com, *www.mayega.com*

- Rev. Dr. Michael Milner, Ph.D., Awakened Advanced Oneness Trainer, Oneness Meditator, Sacred Chambers Facilitator: Clearwater, Fla.; Michael@floweringheart.org, *www.onenessflorida.org, www.floweringheart.org*

- Mary O'Neill, Awakened Advanced Oneness Trainer: Los Angeles, Calif.; mary.grace.oneill@gmail.com

- Rev. Kristin Panek, Awakened Advanced Oneness Trainer, Sacred Chambers Facilitator: Downers Grove, Ill.; kristinpanek@gmail.com, *www.floweringheartcenter.org, www.mytruevoice.org, www.meetup.com/onenesschicago.com*

- Tazdeen (Taz) Rashid, Oneness Trainer: Skokie, Ill.; tazdeenrashid@gmail.com, *www.djtazrashid.com, www.agorahub.com*

- Paula Rosenfeld, Awakened Oneness Trainer: Chicago, Ill; paula@fromtheheartcenter.com, *www.fromtheheartcenter.com, www.meetup.com/onenesschicago.com*

- Rev. Angelika Schafer, Awakened Oneness Trainer, Sacred Chambers Facilitator: N. San Juan, Calif.; *www.angelikahealingmusic.com*
- Catherine Scherwenka, Awakened Advanced Oneness Trainer, Oneness Meditator, Sacred Chambers Facilitator: Global Citizen; Catherine.Scherwenka@gmail.com, *www.catherinescherwenka.com*
- David Tilove, Awakened Oneness Trainer: Laguna Niguel, Calif.; tilove2@att.net, *www.socaloneness.org*

Index

About the Author

Paula Rosenfeld, Awakened Certified Oneness Trainer, is passionately dedicated to helping people become happy, healthy, and fulfilled. She launched her private practice, From The Heart Center, LLC, in 1992. Her vibrational tool kit includes ancient shamanic healing techniques, energy balancing, clairvoyant consultations, coaching, teaching Oneness courses and meditation, and inspiring people through the written word.

Paula graduated from the University of Illinois with a degree in English Literature, has published articles on topics relating to spirituality, and holds additional certifications in mindfulness meditation and wellness coaching. Her shamanic training has been primarily with the Foundation for Shamanic Studies. She's the proud mother of a grown daughter, who has always been her greatest teacher.

As a practitioner of the shamanic methods of Soul Retrieval and Extraction since 1994, Paula has assisted more than 1,000 people and animals in recovering from trauma and connecting with what is sacred to them. Additionally, she leads shamanic journey circles that support direct experiences of healing and guidance through individual communion with spiritual guides.

Paula's awakening in 2013 at Oneness University in India ignited an even deeper desire to assist in the transformation of world consciousness. As a Certified Oneness Trainer, she initiates people to become Deeksha Givers, giving them an opportunity to rapidly grow in awareness and happiness, and to help others grow as well. Through teaching Oneness courses that guide people on how to have good relationships and achieve better health, authenticity, and abundance, Paula is thrilled to work in service of humanity's awakening.

Paula's practice and teaching extend globally. All sessions can be done by phone, Skype, or in person in the Chicago area. Her Website is *www.fromtheheartcenter.com*, and she can be reached at paula@fromtheheartcenter.com.